AF538949

SOCIO-ECONOMIC IDEAS OF NEHRU AND GLOBALISATION

SOCIO-ECONOMIC IDEAS OF NEHRU AND GLOBALISATION

By

DR. S. R. SINGH
Principal, A.N.S. College, Bodh Gaya

DR. M.P. SHRIVASTAVA
Professor, Department of Economics
Magadh University, Bodh Gaya

ANMOL PUBLICATIONS PVT. LTD.
NEW DELHI - 110 002 (INDIA)

ANMOL PUBLICATIONS PVT. LTD.
4374/4B, Ansari Road, Daryaganj
New Delhi - 110 002
Ph.: 23261597, 23278000
Visit us: www.anmolpublications.com

Socio-Economic Ideas of Nehru and Globalisation

First Published 2004

ISBN 81-261-1537-8

PRINTED IN INDIA

Published by J.L. Kumar for Anmol Publications Pvt. Ltd., New Delhi - 110 002 and Printed at Mehra Offset Press, Delhi.

Dedicated

in the memory of

Late (Professor) P.R. Brahmananda

Contents

Preface

Pandit Jawaharlal Nehru belongs to that rare brand of eminent parliamentarians, planners, erude scholars, reputed authors, intellectuals and academics who were in the forefront of Indi's freedom struggle and whose outstanding contributions won independence for this country. Nehru was a true democrat as well as socialist and this combination booked strange to many as observer. Foe him, the two roles were not contradictory rather complementary to each other. Both as a visionary an Statesman, Nehru viewed this process in the spirit of what he called the Indian revolution and the country's economic and political imparatives.

He steered clear of many a controversy but at times had to wage his battle alone. It was Nehru who had to provide, so to say, the colour scheme for the Indian panorama—or for the great mansion of free India. He was one who held the institution of Parliament in the highest esteem. He was a master builder, one of the few architects in his delicate uncommon art of national building. Three passion guided him—passion for freedom, passion for democracy and passion for modernization.

His acute sense of history, his mystic communion with the Indian psyche, his ever-present concern for the relevant, the rational and the progressive and incessant longing for the transformation of this traditional society into a modern polity committed to him to a life long mission for the completion of the gigantic socio-economic revolution in India. The tripartite synthesis was reflected so fully in Nehru's mental makeup, writings, pronouncements political motivations, exertins and policy-decisions, both during struggle for national independence and later during the formative phase of democratic nation-building, that it is in this that singles him out even in the galaxy of the great national leaders as a man who more than others represented more fully and authentically the new enlightened generation of India. Nehru was free from obscuratism, parochialism and dogmatism of any shape and form. He fought casteism and communalism with the vigour which opposed feudal, reactionary and sectarian approaches to politics and social situations. He had an integrated and wholesome perspective of socio-economic change, almost acquiring an ideological over tone.

The commitment of Nehru to the modernization of India, found expression in his attachment to the six guiding principles of national reconstruction namely: (i) in calculation of rationalism and scientific temper in all aspects of life; (ii) secular outlook in politics; (iii) cosmopolitanism in culture; (iv) concern for the use of modern technology and scientific skills for the development of economy; (v) adaption of socialistic principles of Indian conditions for pursuing the objectives of social justice, cohesive economic growth and progressive policies; and (vi) stabilization of the foundation of a participatory, federal democracy that could unite and integrate politically the huge sprawling republic comprising many languages, culture, ethnic groups, religious communities and socio-economic strata. Inspired by these ideals he gave a positive shift and a definite direction to the complex process of building a new India Indeed, herein lies his distinctive contribution as a system builder.

Jawaharlal Nehru was the biggest system builder which India has produced in modern times. He was able to build a system partly because he was the biggest consensus builder. Nobody in the history of India was able to build up such a consensus on majour issues which still holds good and valid :

(a) Participatory democracy working in federal policy; (b) self-reliant; self-generating planned economy attuned to distributive justice; (c) secular egalitarian society; and (d) independent foreign policy.

He was of ten refereed to as a visionary. He was mainly responsible for laying the foundation of our industrial base because he believed that it was only with a progressive industrial base that India could also take itself into the 21st century. He also placed emphasis on science and modern technology, which has enabled India to put a satellite in orbit and, industrially, take its place among the first eight industrial nations of the world.

India demanded a new model of growth—a model that should reconcile the universal experience of mankind at similar stage of development with 'pecific' situational conditioning and requirements of the Indian people. And in quest of this model Nehru had bent his energies. Yet, it may be added that Nehru himself might not have preferred to call it a 'model' of a 'pattern', or even a 'design' for he was averse to the stylized rigidity that is inbuilt in academic terminologies.

From a very early age, Jawaharlal Nehru showed signed signs of a sharp intelligence, high measure of sensivity and natural inclination to react sharply to injustice. He hated injustice in any form and in any field of life. During his educational career in England and subsequent frequent visits to Britain and other European nations he came into close contact with the leaders of Fabian Society and such intellectuals as Professor Laski of London School of Economics. Consequently, he accepted the "socialistic approach of life" and he became committed believer in Socialism and concept of an egalitarian society. When he first returned to India he was shocked by poverty and degradation from which vast mass of Indian people was suffering under the British rule. He held the view that the 200 years of British Imperial domination had ruined the people of India politically economically and culturally. The art and the crafts for which India was famous in the many parts of the world were gradually eliminated by killing impact of machine-made goods. He arrived at he conclusion that the abolition of social and economic thrawldom could be achieved only through the path of socialism.

Meanwhile, the philosophy of Marxism seems to have influenced his mind in no uncertain degree. Infact, he declared publicly more than once that the history of the Industrial Revolution in the West could be properly explained only in terms of Marxism. The Bolshevik Revolution of October, 1919 in Russia after the end of First World War attracted him powerfully.

Despite his great respect for Marxism ideology, he did not believe in communism. He was fully conscious of the inadequacies of the communist philosophy as a comprehensive way of life. His study of Marxism gave him a deep insight into capital-labour relations and a profound understanding of the phenomenon of class conflict and class struggle generated by the inhuman exploitation of labour, including low paid female and child labour in workshops and factories in most countries of the world.

He condemned the acquisitive and competitive society and wanted it to be replaced by a co-operative society where people do not think in terms of individual profits but would rather strive for common good where there is less exploitation. His concept of social welfare included almost every thing that one can think of spiritually, culturally, politically, economically and socially, this concept covers the entire field of human activities and relationship.

He initiated the economic development of the country through a series of Five Year Plans, public sector and through the method of trial and error. He was sure that with the passage of every Five Year Plan, better thing would prevail and each plan would stand to benefit from the success of failure of the previous one. He was, however, sure that planning was essential and without it there would be economic anarchy.

"Socialistic pattern of society" was one of the major objectives of his economic policy and a part of his vision. He was indeed, the symbol of hope and aspiration to the people of the country. He was never a student of Economics but Nehruvian socio-economic approach expounded a belief in man and commitment to liberty. He gave new emphasis to the interlinking of economics and politics of capitalism and imperialism. He was optimistic and his belief was a product of pure reason, which erased the darker aspect of Indian situation as he had immense faith in the capacity of people.

Nehru was the firm believer of mixed economy approach in planned development of India. He supported this model of development in the interest of quicker growth of the economy and for providing social justice. But unfortunately, mixed economy concept has failed in India.

Centralised planning and its tool in a mixed economy like ours brought about rapid economic growth but its fruits have not reached judiciously to the larger number of masses. Indian economy, society, culture etc. are at present passing through the crisis and turmoil. A moral degradation has set in all walks of life. Our socio-economic problems have primarily been caused due to erosion of ethics or value among people an the leaders.

He advocated for the improvement of quality of socio-economic life of human being because human attitudes, behaviour and motivation and values are crucial determinants of economic and social well-being. He also argued for land reforms to improve agricultural productivity and to establish a relation between work and income. He did not advocate complete socialization or capitalization or nationalisation of all means of production, distribution consumption and the exchange. His economic ideas were mainly circumscribed by is paradigm.

He was the great supporter of globalisation because to him economic nationalism was governed by dogma. He was also pioneer in sponsoring a modern out look for restructuring and reconstructing the set up of Indian economy. As a new experiment for the global economic movement he considered his ideas on democratic planning. Population problem was considered by him as a global problem. His ideas of progressive taxation, principle of ability to pay, problem of capital formation, deficit financing, internal debt, foreign assistance, international institutions, land reform, human resource development, stages of economic growth etc., are still significant. His views on laissez-faire policy, capitalism, profit-motive, free economy state interference, planned and unplanned free enterprises, big-philosophy, democracy under laissez-faire, failures of capitalism, socio-economic structure, position of poor consumers, democracy and capitalism, agriculture land reforms, division of land, Zamindars, cottage and small scale industries, infrastructure, khadi industries, community development, co-operative farming, capital formation, sources of capital, pattern of taxation population planning, problem of production and distribution, poverty and unemployment, 'socialistic pattern of society', human paracites, touchability, public sector, public accountability, on planning, formation of National Development Council and Planning Commission, democratic planning, perspective planning, balanced planning etc. are still useful and highly appreciable and valuable even in the perspective of globalisation and liberalization.

New India has proved to the world that despite its chaotic political scenario, imbalanced wealth distribution, redundant bureaucracy, past baggage of Nehruvian socialism, and its sundry other problems, it can implement sustainable economic restructuring in the world's most populous democracy. India has the potential, but the strong economic performance of recent years requires continuing efforts to deepen it and make it work. In evitably, the winds of liberalization that swept through the nation opened a veritable Pandora's box with far-reaching implications for human resource management. In the pre-liberalisation period, India had pursued a short sighted policy in the name of self-reliance, blocking out the rest of the world in the manufacturing and service sector. Similarly employment issues are tremendous issues for both Nehruvian as well as non-Nehruvian era.

In course of writing this book we received numerous help and constant co-operation both directly and indirectly from many corners as such we express our deep sence of gratitude to all such eminent personalities who helped us much. We are grateful to Hon'ble Mr. Sompal, Member, Planning Commission and Ex Union Minister for Agriculture, Govt. of India; Hon'ble Mr. Lal Muni Choubey, M.P. (Lok Sabha); Hon. Nitish Kumar, Union Minister for Railways; Govt. of India; Dr. Abhimanu Singh, Hon. Vice Chancellor, Magadh University, Dr. Sudama Singh, Prof. & Head, Deptt. of Economics, M.U., Dr. B.N. Singh, Dr. L.S. Singh, Dr. Narendra Pd. of Economics, M.U., Bodh-Gaya for their good wishes. We are thankful to all who have helped us directly or indirectly.

We are thankful to Mr. J.L. Kumar Proprietor and Sri Kirpal D. Joshi for getting it published in such an excellent get up.

Dr. Sita Ram Singh

Dr. M.P. Shrivastava

1

Introduction

The purpose of this book is to attempt for filling a gap in the field of Nehruvian studies especially in terms of present age of globalisation and liberalisation. For his unique role as an economist, social scientist, reformer, builder and architect of modern democracy in building parliamentary democracy, parliamentary traditions, conventions, and procedures had not received due attentions from the scholars.

A well dressed man with his red rose tucked on his coat, Pt. Jawaharlal Nehru was an embodiment of sacrifice to his credit. He was a dynamic personality and a statesman of world calibre. He had established himself throughout the world as an attractive, brillant and a progressive idealist. In fact, he was all human which made him a very lovable person. He was not only an astute politician but had become the soul of India. His greatest contribution was his rentless effort to keep the flame of freedom burnign and alive in the hearts of all men and women in India not only of political freedom but of economic and social freedom as well. He tried to evolve good parliamentary conventions and traditions. He treated the opposition always with all the courtesy due to them.

Pandit Jawaharlal Nehru was the prime artificer of modern India and of her socio-economic-political-cultural and religious system of representataive parliamentary democracy.

His contribution to the evolution of India's socio-economic-political system was unique. It was Pandit Jawaharlal Nehru who built brick by brick, the infrastructure and the edifice of India and the institution called the Parliament of India. Himself an erudit scholar and a reputed author, Pandit Nehru inspired many intellectuals and academics. Volumes have been written on him on his life and works, his Prime Ministership, his foreign policy and more recently on his active role in constitution making. Unfortunately, however, very little research seems to have been undertaken so far as his role in building socio-economic and political base in terms of globalisation and present economic reform and the great institution of parliament and establishing loftly parliamentary traditions conventions and procedures.

Long before the freedom for foreign rule became a reality way back in 1936, Jawaharlal Nehru as President of the Indian National Congress had declared that ultimate objective was "the establishment of a democratic state" a sovereign state of India which would promote and foster 'full democracy' and user in an era of "new social and economic order". The dominant urges of the Indian nation, he then observed, were nationalism, freedom and social justice. Throughout his public career whether as the leader of Indian nationalism or as the Prime Minister of India, he laid stress on the validity of these concepts, for buildings a modern democratic polity in India.

Nehru was described as a "gentle colossus". It was his innate gentleness and his gentlemanliness that made Nehru an ornament to the nation. His adherence to the doctrine of "Panchsheel" in foreign affairs in well known. He also contributed another set of five doctrines such as:

(i) Planned Development

(ii) Parliamentary Democracy

(iii) Socialism

(iv) Mixed Economy

(v) The Scientific Temper.

In transforming political democracy into economic democracy, Nehru was faced with a reverse problem in comparison to the west. He used to say that in the west industrial revolution had preceeded political revolution. In India we had political revolution first and the essential task was to bring about in an industrial and economic revolution. What Nehru meant by that was that the political freedom. We had achieved was to be translated into economic freedom. Planned economy was the instrument Nehru employed for the realisation of his philosophy of political democracy. Nehru was essentially a man of the modern age inbued with a deep scientific spirit. He had a dual task before him of boosting up the country's economy and of modernising the country and pushing at forward from the bullock cart age to the Jet and space age. He had to do this within the parameters of a democratic form of government.

Acharya J.B. Kripalani while paying tribute to Nehru's memory in Parliament, stated, "He wanted to bring about in India an industrial revolution after the industrial revolution in the west. This was a stupendous task. It was a harden task than the fight for national liberation. Such a social transformation has been attempted in history throughout the world by methods that are cruel, arbitrary and ruthless. But he wanted to bring about this transformation by non-violence and through democratic ways.

Nehru's faith in parliamentary democracy flowed from his vision of political democracy. Through his efforts, the country has a democratic constitution, which enshrined as one of its laudable objectives "equality of status and opportunity, justice, social, economic, political and dignity of the individual, and unity of the nation".

Thus, nationalism, socialism and secularism constituted the main pillars of the edifice of democracy that Nehru sought to build. In whatever Nehru did or thought, democracy was the dominant idea. His socialism was democratic socialism, and his planning was also democratic planning. His concept of socialism did not conform to the type of socialism prevalent in the socialist countries. In India he wanted to have a socialist pattern of society in keeping with the country's democratic framework. For India's rapid economic development. Nehru introduced planning, but his planned economy was not modelled after Soviet Union or other socialist countries. A planned economy under a democratic political system was a new experiment.

Jawaharlal Nehru had made a detailed and exhanstive study of capitalism, socialism, democratic planning, economic liberalisation, private property, land reform, foreign trade, agriculture industry. Communication, science and technology, modernisation, distribution of income and wealth, poverty, un-employment and national income. He studied the effects of second World war on the Indian economy and how the problems arising therefrom were tackled by the then alien government. Although there was no declared economic policy, yet after a critical examination of the economic activities undertaken by the government he concluded that the "Government war time economic policy has been one of low production, high degree of scarcity for the civilian population and the use of inflationary method for obtaining the bulk of rupee finance requised by His Megesty's Government. Then Nehru explained what the war time economic policy of the country ought to have been".

It was in this connection that he put forward the following suggestions:

(i) Production must be increased to its maximum for this purpose all the economic resources of the country should be fully mobilised.

(ii) The diversion of economic resources from the civilian to the military use must not involve the use of inflationary methods.

(iii) Economic resources diverted for military purposes should be most efficiently organised and put to the maximum use.

He also examined the problems and policies of the post war economy. He enlisted the changes brought about by the war as reduction in imports, emergence of India as a creditor nation, increase in public expenditure rise in price and employment level etc. According to Pt. Nehru, the permanent economic problems of the Indian economy were related to poverty, food supply, unemployment and under employment and industrialisation. He suggested some important remedies for the improvement of the economic policy:

(a) Indian agriculture should be rehabilitated.

(b) The economic requirements of different regions should be paid due attention to.

(c) The objectives of providing employment should be long range.

(d) There should be no abrupt transition from war time to peace time economy.

(e) Unhindered imports of consumer goods should not be permitted.

(f) War time control should be relaxed gradually, and demobilisation should be effected by stages.

(g) Labour problems should be solved efficiently by establishing labour exchanges and machinery for the settlement of industrial disputes and provision of social security.

In this connection he has stated that the objective is the promotion of higher standard of living, full employment and condition of economic and social progress and development in the countries concerned, and the manner for achieving it is a sound, efficient and fuller utilisation of manpower, natural resources, energy and capital. To him, in underdeveloped economies real income continues to remain low: there is economic stagnation. Voluntary savings do not increase part pasm with the increase in investment. As a result, these ensures a gulf between savings and investment which begins to close only with economic development and capital formation. His these ideas have been widely supported by Prof. Amabtya Sen, Novel Prize winner Economist.

Nehru discusses of economic development in a free society, in which the common man is able to function with freedom. In such a society, he gets an opportunity of improving his condition of work. He should democratic freedom to have an elected government, independent judiciary, freedom of association, speech, press, movement and occupation.

To him, what is essential for economic development is an increase in savings and investment, a desire for larger output and lower cost on the part of employers and executives and industrial discipline on the part of workers without which production can't increase. The most dynamic factor is the rate of capital accumulation. An increase in the saving and investment becomes possible on account of an increase in the potential development surplus which accrues from increased production.

He was of the opinion that the distribution of surplus determines the rate of economic growth. This surplus is divided among the saver, employer, worker and government. In achieving development the conscious and disciplined participation of the masses is urgently needed. The new society under democratic socialism can't be organised without hard work, discipline and austere living.

According to Pt.Nehru Indian economy is predominantly agricultural where capital equipment is low and standard of technical knowledge applied to technical production is vastly inferior to that in the west.

The assumption of a closed economy, no more holds good. Indian economy has been globalised. Indian trade both is terms of value & volume and in terms of composition and direction is undergoing a sea change.

Planning ensures rapid economic development which can't be satisfied with fulfilment of target and increase in production. It has, necessarily, to ensure equitable distribution and reduction of poverty. Both Gandhi and Nehru influenced Indian planning, but the latter's impact was greater than former, though philosophically both played their role in shaping the Indian Planning for development.

His base is so strong and hence allowed many modification in building the super structure with modern refinements. His other great quality is conceiving a vision to create institutions of higher learning and research in economics for turning out the best quality thinkers and researchers in the field of economics for the development of Indian economy. The intellectual economist in him as an original thinker laid many strategic roads methods of development.

The lucidity of presentation of ideas, the idealism he preached and practised as an economist, statesman, social reformer, the objective way in which he selected persons and used them for the development of Indian economy, he established through quality work, the solutions suggested for solving economic problems, the critical approach evolved to study the issues and problems, the new strategy suggested for balanced development (with justice) of regions by proper utilisation of resources physical, natural and human and the active dynamism provided by him as a leader of excellence are recognised by all to make him a man of greatness and eminance. He was very active as a thinker, administrator, leader, statesman, social reformer, master builder of parliamentary democracy, architect of modern India and institution builder till his last days and did best service to India and the field of economics in the world. He was a great oretor with skills to make the audience attentive and acceptable with lucid and analytical presentation of any economic issue or problem facing India.

Jawaharlal Nehru was also the father of planning and firm believer of mixed economy. He opted for middle path due to his belief in socialistic pattern of development, by providing commanding heights to the public sector and at the same time encouraging private sector through assigning appropriate role in the development process. If rapid development of society is the goal, it is inevitable for the public sector to play a dominant role as viewed by Nehru. Since private sector evinces interest only in field of giving profit, rapid development will be jeopardised if they are entrusted with development work. Moreover, China and Russia have attained rapid growth through socialist path. Core sectors like steel, coal, electricity, telephone, file communications, railways and infrastructure facilities like roads, ports, navy airways etc. have to be developed by public sector and non-core sectors by private sector. Thus, came into prominence the mixed economy approach in planned development of India. According this line of approach and moved by its relevance Nehru supported this model of development in the interest of quicker growth of the economy and for providing justice.

To achieve the objective of economic growth with social justice, an integrated and wholesome approach to development must be applied that would ensure policies factors necessary for a parliamentary democracy as well as economic factors relevant to growth; it should also provide socio-cultural factors required for both growth and to justice because the latter would Counteract effectively the influence put by vested interest, the composition and bias of the power structure and all the non-economic parameters that would obstruct the path to socialist transformation. In this context it must be realised that freedom possessed by private enterprise has not helped the poor but helped in strengthening of the vested interest in the rural economy and the creation of a powerful agricultural class that had its impact on the rural power structure against rural poor and social justice they deserve.

Thus, mixed economy followed did not ensure socio-cultural environment and factors that would facilitate correct usage of political freedom for gaining economic justice from economicgrowth. In other words, political justice is not sufficient to obtain economic justice without proper support and impact of social and cultural factors relevant social justice. Mixed economy has failed in India for its imroper conditioning under unhelpful factors.

Centralised planning and its tools in mixed economy brought about rapid growth of the economy but its fruits have not reached judiciously to the larger number of masses.

The Indian economy, society and culture are, at present going through various crisis and turmoil. A moral degeneration has set in all walks of life. Our socio-economic problems have primarily been caused due to erosion of ethics or value among people and leaders and not due to external factors. According to Prof. V.K.R.V. Rao "And while capital and technology are both essential for growth, an equally important element is the way the human factor is harnessed for the purpose. Literacy, education, skills as also health and nutrition, all these undoubtedly add to the efficacy of the human factor. But the human being is more than mixture of mind and matter". According to Nehru human has a value. He has a soul, or if you prefer, a conscience. He dreams of a new and better world, and his dreams have a force and a power that is more than yielded by a many millions of kilowatts of electric power or many thousands of lows of the most conplicated machinery. Efficiency of human factor in production processes depends on fair factors; physical organisational, mantal and psychological of these, the last two are extremely curcial.

Once again, it needs to be stressed that mere physical and organisational superiority of human resources would not necessarily promote economic growth and all round development.

The attitudes and values that human being demonstrate are extremely important in influencing the quality of economic and social life. Unless there is an honest urge among the people who are both means and ends of production process it is difficult to achieve plan objectives and other goals. Nehru rightly stated that development is essentially a psychological phenomenon.

Since, human attitudes, behaviour motivation and values are crucial determines of economic and social well being, every attempt must be made to improve the quality of these ingredients. And thus, accordingly calls for not only spread of education but also initiation of institutional changes.

In order to motivate the vast masses in rural economy

viz. farmers in improving agricultural productivity Nehru talked of land reforms, he urged the need for establishing a relation between work and income.

On work culture, it may be stated that in public sector, is abysmally poor. The Indian workers egged on by militant trade unions and political parties have increasingly restive. They demand for higher wages and other benefits but often fail to realize that they also have a duty to the citizens and the state. It is thus, essential that right from the start of the process of deleberate economic development, the connection between work and income must be built into psychology of the people including not only the classes but also the masses.

His socio-economic ideas are historically very significant and relevant. His deep studies in socialism, capitalism, marxism, his views on class-war, private property, socialistic pattern of society, nationalism, internationalism, socio-economic concepts, democratic, physical and financial planning swaraj, taxation, capital formation, new economic order, stages of economic conflicts sbetween capitalism, and democracy, communalism, Indian market conditions, decline in agriculture and small scale industries, awareness of peasants and industrial protection, growth of leftist philosophy, right of individual, socio-economic issues of capitalism, socialism, are still very useful. His economic ideas were mainly circumscribed by his pragmatism. He did not believe in the liberal school of economics, though, in politics he was attached to the concept of liberty. He did not approve the theory of laissez-faire or non-intervention in industries, trade and commerce. He did not advocate socialisation or nationalisation of all means of production, distribution consumption and exchange, he readily tolerated the private sector in the transitional phase.

He, being progressive and pragmatic in his outlook had picked up the practical side and accepted the concept of 'mixed-economy'. He was the great supporter of globalisation and internationalism.

He suggested for the globalisation and internationalism of today and for acting globally. To him, economic nationalism was governed by a dogma. The economic nationalism was an out of worn creed and internationalism mates more and more to reality. He was, as such, pioneer in sponsoring a modern out-look for restructuring and reconstructing the Indian economic set up. He considered his ideas on democratic planning as a new experiment for the global economic movement. To him, democratic planning was the only weapon for killing the basic evils of socio-economic system. He pointed out that there was a supplementary and complementary relationship among agriculture, industries, small-scale and cottage industries, trade and commerce.

Besides, Jawaharlal Nehru desired to build up swaraj right from the village with adequate necessary powers, functions and resources. So far as 'new economic order' is concerned, he gave priority to the quality of human resources which can build up the wealth of nation as well as its cultural and moral progress.

As regards, public finance, he favoured progressive direct taxation and the principle of ability to pay. He deeply and widely probed the problem of capital formation and supported to finance various schemes for economic development through taxation, deficit financing, internal debt but not beyond limit. He further examined pros and cons of foreign assistance. Population problem was considered by him as the world problem which eats up the world resources. Consequent upon this he firmly advocated family planning as an official policy.

Nehru made it clear that under laissezfaire policy the economy can not run progressively. He was against profit motive though, he advocated for incentives. He was against unplanned enterprise and he opposed concentration of wealth in the individual health. He clearly stated that an economy can not make any progress at all with an unplanned 'free-enterprise'. Individual liberty in the laissez-faire economy was a mere myth which was called as the law of jungle and 'pigphilosophy' by carlyle under this system democracy was only political democracy and not economic democracy which was quite unable to solve industrial and agricultural problems. According to him democracy and liberty have no existance with equality. He tried to establish balance between centralisation of powers and authority of states. According to him apart from protecting the individual from foreign enemies or internal disorder. State had the duty of undertaking provision of equal opportunities for the progress of education and health, economic and social justice and overall progress.

To Nehru agricuture and land reform are still very significant. Agriculture is not only an occupation or a business rather it is a tradition and way of life. It is the matter of all industries and maintenance of human life and maintainer of human life. It provides food for all whether people or cattle. It also provides large proportion of India's export. According to him the problem of land reform is the fundamental problem of rural economy.

Socialism, according to him in India is quite irrelevant unless the life of primary producer is made economically better and socially secure. He observed that the reform have a peculiar significance and he considered it more scientific and revolutionary and initiated a number of notable steps for the welfare of the cultivators.

He favoured public sector and argued that without public sector India can't fulfil her various socio-economic objectives as it occupies key role in our socio-economic activities and it is regarded as an engine of growth and social justice. To him public sector is quite essential for the creation and development of infrastructure, checking concentration of wealth, creation of enormous employment opportunities, promotion of balance regional development. As such, he was in favour of enforcement of accountability from top to bottom through parliamentary ministerial and audit agencies, he played key role in promoting parliamentary committees like Public Accounts Committee, Estimates Committee and Committee of Public undertakings with the help of former speaker Honourable Mr. G.V. Mavalankar.

His approach towards planning was pragmatic and practical. He deeply studied the economic planning of Soviet Russia and played key and dynamic role in the formulation and execution of Indian planning. He was plan minded Bombay Plan, 1944. People's Plan of M.N. Roy, the Gandhian Plan. Planning Commission and National Development Council all are directly related to him. Planning commission and the National Development Council are his great gifts; multilevel planning, district planning, physical and financial planning, democratic planning, flexible and rigid planning, balanced planning, human aspects of planning are indeed his main contributions with regard to planning.

Thus, his all the ideas relating to socio-economic planning, public sector, parliament, new economic reform (globalisation and liberalisation) etc. are very pertinent and useful even at the present deteriorating and gloomy set up. In this book all these issues have been carefully studied and examined for filling the gap in the field of studies relating to Pandit Jawaharlal Nehru in various chapters.

2

Economic Views of Nehru

This chapter is an attempt for evaluating the main economic ideas of Pandit Jawaharlal Nehru in the context of present day economic reform and globalisation initiated by Dr. Manmohan Singh the then Finance Minister of India under the Prime Ministership of Mr. P.V. Narasimha Rao since 1991. His economic ideas are still relevant and can play a very significant part in accelerating growth process not only in India but in the entire third world.

While the case of economic reforms may take good note of the diagnosis that India has too much government interference in some fields, it ignores the fact that India also has insufficient and ineffective government activities in many other fields including basic education health care, social security, land reform and the phenomenon of social change. This criteria too contributes to the persistence of widespread deprivation, economic stagnation and social inequality.

The main economic ideas of Jawaharlal Nehru can be studied under following headings i.e. Nehru's ideas on:

(a) Economic Liberalisation

(b) Capitalism

(c) Agriculture and Land Reform

(d) Cottage and Small Scale Industries and Rural Industrialisation

(e) Khadi Industries

(f) Community Development

(g) Co-operative Principles

(h) New Economic Reforms and Globalisation

(i) Capital Formation

(j) Human Resource Development

(k) Pattern of Taxation

(l) Stages of Economic Growth

(m) Population Planning

All these ideas are very significant dispite some basic drawbacks. As such, it would be in the fitness of thing to examine all these ideas of Pt. Jawaharlal Nehru the master builder of Indian Parliamentary Democracy, planning and modern economy. Through these ideas, he has been treated as the true democrat and architect of modern Indian economy virtually it was he who started the industrial agricultural, transport and commercial revolutions in Indian economy.

A. Economic Liberalisation and Nehru

The liberal school of economic philosophy was under the dominating influence of the doctrine of Laissez-faire, more than a century ago. It means 'let things along' applied to any view economic or political which favour individualism and oppose state intervention. This concept called as 'Police State' or 'The Original State' according to Jawaharlal Nehru, was very simple state in which particularly speaking all that the state had to do was to protect the individually from a foreign enemy or another tribe. From that developed concept of what might be called as police state. A state preserved law and order protected its citizens from foreign enemies, and realised taxes to carry on its business. For the rest it was left to the individual or the group.[1]

According to Nehru one notable book came out in England in the second half of the eighteenth century known as "Wealth of Nations" of so called 'Father of Economics', Adam Smith. It was a book on political economy of in which Economics was dealt by smith in this book in a scientific way and tried to find natural laws which governed economics. In the worlds of Pt. Nehru.

"Economics .... deals with the management of the income and expenditure of the people or a country as a whole, of what they produce and what they consume and their relations with each other and other countries and people".[2]

Smith believed that full liberty should be given for the development of industry so that natural laws might not be interfered with. Actually, this was the beginning of the doctrine of 'Laissez-faire'. It was only due to fact that when every body worked for his own self, interest, somehow the totality of such work lead to public good.

Laissez-faire Policy

According to Nehru the doctrine of Laissez-faire laid stress on the theoretical freedom of each individual to work according to this bent in the hope that he would try from self-interest to better himself in every way and thus, society would progress.

Explaining the behaviour of English employers of the 18th Century in England Nehru wrote about Laissez-faire that under this new philosophy they preferred their business without interference from government.

In the other words, this notion means non-interference of state in economic affairs, freedom of economic pursuit, freedom of contract, the right to chose any occupation to accumulate capital to use or not use or transfer capital and inputs and right or inheritance of property.

Basis of Laissez-faire Policy

But according to him this doctrine was more critical in nature than more explanation as Laissez-faire form of economic policy is based on the basic institutions like:

(i) Unlimited acquisitiveness or profit motive;

(ii) free enterprise in a state of perfect conception;

(iii) monopoly of property in the material means of production;

(iv) Laissez-faire relationship between state and its economic and civic functions and individualism.

Acquisitive Society

Its distinguishing work was acquisitiveness. It was always out to acquaire and hold and then acquire again. Individuals tried to do so, and so did nations. The society that grew up under this system was therefore, called on acquisitive society.

To Nehru, this acquisitive society which grew in the days of Laissez-faire economy is no longer suited to the present age. "Personally, I think that the acquisitive society, which is the base of capitalism is no longer suited to the present age. It may have been suitable in an earlier period and, undoubtedly capitalism has great gain to its credit, but the world has outgrown that stage.[3]

Moreover, an acquisitive society, based on profit motive, appeared to Nehru out of date in the new world that is growing up, it does not mean that there should be no incentives. Incentives will always be necessary though, they may not be confined to financial benefits."[4]

Profit Motive and Nehru

As regards profit motive which was at the work very strongly in the Laissez-faire economy, the conception of Jawaharlal Nehru was against this. To quote him "The whole system protects and gives every scope to man's predatory instinct, it encourages some finer instincts no doubt, but much more so the baser instimets of man. Success means the knocking down of others and mounting on their *vanquished selves*".[5] Even in the context of world today, such a motive is becoming increasingly not only wrong from the economic point of view but a vulgar thing from any sensitive point of view, so changes are bound to come."[6]

However, he did not rule out profit entirely. It may continue in the limited sense if it was good on moral grounds. But in larger sense, it may come more and more into conflict with the new idea of socialist state. That conflict would go on. He perhaps wanted elimination of profit motive in society and its replacement by a spirit of social service, co-operation for consumption instead of profit.[7]

Nehru on Free Economy

Free enterprise also derived, from Laissez-faire economy, is a purely hypothetical proposition. Under this conditions, the most urgent wants of the owners of income would be satisfied. Thus, Nehru has stated.

"What is called 'free enterprise' will never appeal to the masses of our people; it will lead to the use of our resources often/ for purposes that are not of primary importance. It will mean the exploitation of the profit in which the individual may be interested but not society as a whole."[8]

Pt. Nehru initiating the parliamentary debate in the Lok Sabha on May 23, 1956 on the Second Five Plan argued,

"I am quite certain that with an unplanned free enterprise approach, we can't make any progress at all. If there is any progress it will be lopsided. We can put up factories, here and there but it will result only in riches here and greater poverty there.[9]

He further stated "We want to avoid large concentration of wealth in individual hands. Such a concentration is a bad for society event though that wealth may sometimes be used for good purposes.[10] According to him, "absence of state control means cut throat competition, chaos and disaster."[11]

It was only due to fact that the tendency has been for the monopoly of wealth and property to pass into a limited hands. The few persons who have the monopoly of capital really dominate the sence. By their method of business and by virtue of the fact that they have large sum of money at their command, they can for instance squeeze out the little shopkeeper, without giving the slightest compensation, they can crush him out of existence together.[12]

The main central idea behind the philosophy of free enterprise is to stress on the production only, but the production itself does not solve the problem of human society. As such, there must be proper distribution also as he remarked.

"But it became increasingly evident that production by itself does not solve our problems or lead to happiness and contentment".[13] According to Nehru problem of equitable distribution and the right use of what is produced has become important, without this the old tussle between the 'haves' and have-nots may become acuter.

State Interference Laissez-faire Economy

Consequent upon this, state interference at this stage is must according to him.[14] Today, every thing is governed by the development of Science and Technology, the idea of

Laissez-faire theory etc. is almost considered at the verge of absurdity except by a few who earn profit greatly under it at the cost of many.[15]

He further written that a nation as a whole shall assume the responsibility of the economy instead of leaving it at the mercy of the self styled messiahs. However, Nehru was ready to tolerate private enterprise in the transitional period only and due to scarcity of resources and not to upset any thing which is working. He did not desire to be of Laissez-faire variety of free enterprise. The private enterprise shall be subjected to regulation and control of the state in the social and national interest. To quote him,

"It is undoubtedly useful so far as our country is concerned, we wish to encourage it but the dominance, it exercised throughout the world during a certain period is no more".[16] There was no conflict among them at all according to him, some people feel that private enterprise should be given full and unrestricted scope. But there can be no unrestricted scope and there can be no such unrestricted private enterprise and the state has to intervene on a big scale. Even in U.S.A. we find progressive socialisation and public utilities and the like are going on.

Planned and Unplanned Free-enterprises

Nehru was quite certain that with an "unplanned free-enterprise" approach we can't make any progress at all. If there is any progress, it will be lopsided.

He was convinced that planned and controlled efforts bring greater production than the unplanned free enterprize. The total wealth production of the country will not be as great as through planned effort. That is a patent fact requires no proof.

The news of those who believe wholly in free enterprise is a state view or is a very slowly changing view. According to him, "World conditions today create forces which compel a country to progress in a certain direction, whether it wants to or not, 'Laissez-faire variety of free enterprise is 'something which does not exist anywhere in the world.[17]

The 19th century individualism insisted upon the reproduction of power and authority of the state to the minimum. English businessmen, the leaders of the new industries in those days, were not much interested in high democratic principles and the people right to liberty. But they discovered that great liberty for the people was good for business. Laissez-faire form of economic policy had tried to solve the problem. But as Nehru observed, liberty of the individual in the Laissez-faire economy was a mere myth itself. The theory of individual freedom failed. In this context, there was no slavery. The law was all in favour of the employer.

Nehru on Pig-Philosophy

The Laissez-faire variety of economic policy brought the law of the jungle. Carlyle called it as 'Pig-philosophy; The poor fellows had little to say in the matter. It was the successful manufacturers at the top who wanted no interference with their success in the name of foolish sentiment of liberty.

However, a quite convenient philosophy was developed that the poor were necessary for society. Thus, it was quite virtuous to pay low wages. If higher wages were paid the poor would try to have a good time and not work hard enough.

Democracy under Laissez-faire

Democracy under the Laissez-faire is political democracy not economic democracy and deals with the political aspect of liberty and stresses on a theoretical freedom of each individual. It offers no solution of the industrial problems that were existing.

Democracy and liberty have no meaning without equality. Equality can't be established so long as the principal instruments of production are privately owned. Private ownership of these means of production thus comes in the way of real democracy:[18] Therefore, new emphasis was given to the 'watch word, Laissez-faire' "Let everyone work with all high might". The liberal state of 19th century was gradually replaced by the social service of the 20th century. It again joins the ideal of liberty to that of equality and this in the name of social justice. This obviously, leads the modern state to grow more and more centralised. Nehru added.

"You can't escape centralised authority, whether it is of the state, whether it is of the big corporation whether it is of the trade union or whether it is of any group. They all go on being centralised authority".[19]

But now all centralisation is a sight encroachment on the freedom of the individual. We want to preserve the freedom of individual, and at the same time we can't escape centralisation in modern society. According to Nehru establishing balance the two is the real problem in Indian economy. He tried to establish balance between centralisation extension of power and authority of the state and individual freedom. State can't do without a large measure of centralisaion, but on the other hand, individual is highly desirable and there should be some attempt to limit centralisation reducing it to a minimum and so far as it is possible, to centralise the rest.

Nehru desired that the political rights of individual be safeguarded but the constitution of the state. As regards economic question, it is a question of state interference to protect, rather than keeping away.

State, according to him, apart from protecting the individual from foreign enemies or internal disorders, has the duty to undertake to provide him with the opportunities of progress of education, health sanitation generally everything that would give him the opportunity following himself for such work as he is capable of.[20]

Economic Functions of the State

As regards economic functions of the state, he believed, is a flexible policy, especially with regard to his own country, where resources are not abundant, he stated, any project should be a state project. Certain large projects can either be state projects or jointly owned by the state or private enterprise, with a measure to state control, but living a large field for private enterprise.

According to him, there need not be any rigid lines between private sector, public sector and the joint sector. We can see which functions better and more successfully and allow them to develop.[21] To him it was not merely a political resolution. It was a revolution affecting all the various classes and indeed every body.

B. Nehru on Capitalism

The views of Nehru on Capitalism are still very significant. According to him, it was very difficult to define capitalism. Capitalism of a kind had existed in all countries for a long line in different period of history. According to him, certain fundamental characteristics unmistakably distinguish a capitalistic structure of the society from other economic systems. Private initiative and acquisitiveness are the pivot around which a capitalist order clusters.

Forms of Capitalism

Capitalism to him has many forms:-

(i) Financial Capitalism - money lending for profit by charging interest.

(ii) Commercial Capitalism - buying and selling of goods produced with a view to make profit.

(iii) Industrial Capitalism - controlled means of production by few and production of goods by employing labour on wages and then selling it to earn profit.[22]

The financial and commercial capitalism have an importance of their own. But Industrial capitalism is treated an a synonym of capitalism.

Role of Capitalism

In this book 'Glimpses of World History' he has written that "capitalism of a kind had existed in all countries for a long time that is to say industry was carried on with occumulated money. But with the coming of the big machine and industrialism far greater sum of money were required for factory production."[23]

According to him, capitalism owners of the capital, controlled the factories and took profits. With industrialisation capitalism spread all over the world. The Industrial Revolution of the 18th and 19th centuries gave birth to the capitalism. Before this world event, the world has passed through many stages - like the nomadic, the pastoral, the agricultural, the feudal and the commercial. New invention changed the form of productive mechanism, and big machine industries were set up. Thereby productive potentials have increased greatly.

Despite great opposition, Nehru also recognised the contribution of Capitalism.

Capitalism when it came did a log of good.[24] It added vastly to the wealth of the world. Production was geared up because private enterpreneurs risked their capital, and showed initiative in experimenting with new and latest inventions and discoveries.

Profit motive and acquisitiveness have helped in industrialising developing economies of the world. Nevertheless the social conseuquence of classical capitalism have been depressing. As the capitalistic industry was dynamic, it grew bigger and bigger and its hunger was never satisfied. The workers who produced the wealth of industry benefit least from it.

It is not surprising that the peasant in his field and workers in his factory are poor although they produce the food and wealth of the world.[25]

The most remarkable thing about capitalism was indeed, the contrasts it produced and the more at grew the greater were these contrasts; extreme poverty and extreme wealth; slum and sky - scraper; entire state and dependent exploited colony. So capitalism went blindly and ruthlessly forward, leaving many victims in its trail.[26]

He wrote in a 'letter to his daughter', Indira; "it would partly right and partly wrong. Better methods of production have indeed made the world richer. It was strange thing that inspite of more and more wealth, being produced, the poor had remained poor. It is very strange that these classes have grown up in society of people who do not even pretened to do any work and yet take him share of the work of others."[27]

To quote him, "Real history should deal, not with a few individuals here and there, but with the people who make up a nation, who work and by their labour produce the necessaries and luxuries of life and who is a thousand different ways act and react on each other.[28]

Failures of Capitalism

No sound and stable society can be built up on the basis of inequality and injustice or on the exploitation of one class or group by another. This unfair exploitation exists everywhere. But everywhere people have come to realise this and are working hard to get rid of it. The present system has been admittedly a failure and is condemned.

Nehru admitted the failure of capitalism. "Thus, if we survey the world today, we find that capitalism having solved the problem of production, helplessly faces the allied problem of distribution and is unable to solve it."

The greatest stress was laid on production at the early days of capitalism. But it became increasingly evident that production by itself does not solve our problems or lead to happiness and contentment.

The passion for riches for acquisition for more and more wealth tends to corrupt and to create jealousies and conflict. It indeed tends to create greater imbalance. The problem of equitable distribution and utilisation of goods and commodities produced become important. Economic policy can no longer be considered as some interpretation of Nehru's law apart from human considerations or moral issues.

He rightly proclaimed that industrial revolution and capitalism solved the problem of production. They did not solve the problem of the distribution of the new wealth produced. Consequently, the old tussle between haves and have nots not only remained but it became acuter.

Nehru, being a socialist, wanted production for consumption and not for profit. Although, capitalism stimulated acquisitiveness which did much good also in its earlier stages, yet it seems to have outlived its utility according to him. The profit motive inevitably leads to conflict. The whole system protects and gives every scope to man's predatory instincts it encourages some finer instimates no doubt, but much more so the baser instincts of man.

Socio-Economic Structure

He further stated, "Our economy and social structure have out-lived their day and it has become a matter of urgent necessity for us to refashion them so that they may promote the happiness of all our people in things materials and spiritual. We have to aim deliberately at a social philosophy which seeks a fundamental transformation of this structure, at a society which is not dominated by the urge for private profit and by individual greed and in which there is fair distribution of political power.[29]

Position of Poor Consumers

Thus, the poor consumers become a mere pawn in the simister game of exploitation and he accepts the dictates of kings of industries with spirit of resignation. In his words, "The growth of capitalist industry brought many changes. Capitalism functioned on a bigger and bigger scale. It was more profitable and more efficient for big concerns to functions than small ones. Consequent upon this huge combines trusts grew up, controlling whole industries and they swallowed up the small independent producers and factories."[30] It gains more power and starts casting their injurious shadows over small business concerns. They are pressed into submission. Either the small units of production merge themselves into huge combines or work in utter subserviency to them. Therefore, myth of unlimited opportunities for the small enterpreneur in a 'Laissez-faire' economy receives a set back.

Evil Effects

Since, monopolies are formed to reduce competition, these follow restrictive policies in matters of production to maintain high oppressive prices. The evil effects of monopolies are not confined to economic field only. It is a hard reality that if the state does not own or at least control the means of production and distribution, the state itself tends to be controlled by king of industry. The powerful combines and co-operation dominated governments. It does not militate only against the proper functioning of the economic system, but it also endangers existence of democracy itself.

Democracy & Capitalism

Democracy and capitalism grew up together in the 19th century but they were not mutually campaitible. There was a basic ontradiction between them for democracy laid stress on the power of the many, while capitalism gave real power to the few. Liberty and democracy have no meaning without equality and equality can't be established so long as the principal instruments of production are privately owned. Private ownership of these means of production thus, comes in the way of real democracy.

Relevance of Capitalism

Nehru rightly observed, that industrial capitalism in olden days was acclaimed as the saviour of human being because of modernising production. It increased national wealth tremendously. It also made country after country centres of industries commerce and defence. In fact, it gave new shape to western civilisation, but today it is under disgrace. Capitalism, when it came did a lot of good but now the circumstances have completely been changed. Capitalism plays a very important role in society. During the last century or more it has helped in additing to the wealth of the world. Now it is becoming a terror to further progress.[31]

To Nehru in the global field, capitalism breeds conflicts and colonialism, as it must have global marakets to dump surplus goods. He stated that changing condition in the world demanded a new political and economic orientation and if this does not come soon there is friction and conflict. This gradually leads to revolution in the minds of men. The existing equilibrium having gone, giving place to no other, there is deterioration, reaction and disaster.

As such, it has resulted in recurrent crisis political and

economic, leading to economic and tariff wars as well as political wars on an enormous scale.

Capitalism has outlived its usefulness in the context of present social, aspiration and economic condition. But according to Nehru capitalism is not only system in the world which had to face decadence. Life has never been static rather it is dynamic. Economic systems spring from the dynamics of life and are evolved to meet the prevailing needs and requirements of a community. As society advances, social philosophy changes accordingly. Nothing today represents the final phase of human thought. Every type of human association-political, social or economic has some philosophy at the back of it.

Mixed Economy

Jawaharlal Nehru was founding father of "Mixed Economy" as the choice of the middle way. The policy assumed a sectorial balanced growth of the economy and divided it into public and private sectors. Being directed and regulated properly private sector was to supplement economic activities towards development by maintaining autonomy. And the public sector envisaged a process of economic growth and industrial development under the state ownership and control. To refer the statements of Dr. Hamid, one of the oldest friends of Nehru, "that private enterprise and nationalisation can be equated with democracy and that totalitarianism and nationalisation are the same". According to him, Dr. Hamid either wished to pump for absolute free enterprise or for hundred percent nationalisation.

Nehru felt that Dr. Hamid was "out of touch with" what was happening in the world, and said that there was no country in the world. Where the free enterprise of Dr. Hamid's dream existed, not even in the U.S.A. In the words of Jawaharlal Nehru, "Dr. Hamid motivated him to choose between Soviet Russia and U.S.A. It was a different choices but he was forced to make that he had to find a middle-way through a mixed economy which was neither a "dogma" nor an "axiom" and which could be experimented in Indian conditions.

As P.B. Desai has stated (Planning in India, p. 9, 1951). Apart from the resolution emphasised that cottage and small scale industries had a very important role to play in the national economy and the central government was responsible to investigate how far and in what manner these industries could be co-ordinated and integrated with large scale industries and agreed to establish Cottage Industries Board for fostering their development and gave distinctly "a co-operative bias to the field of industry".

India is an under developed country with limited capital and skill, both in public and private sectors. A steady increase in production is the price requisite, if the basic goal of a higher standard of living for the masses is to be achieved, both public and private capital have important roles to play, to use public funds for nationalisation of existing industry is both short-sighted and foothardy. We must think also beyond the immediate wants of the present and utilise our resources with foresight.

Like a true logician he visualised that an attempt to change the whole economic system, has might have to face a more serious calamity and he imagined a smooth, slow and steady progress. In other words, the aim was to evolve a political system, which was to combine efficiency of administration with individual liberty and an economic structure which could yield maximum production without the operation of private monopolies and the concentration of wealth and could create proper balance between urban and rural economics. Such a social structure could provide an alternative to the acquisitive economy of private capitalisation and the regeneration of a totalitarian state, which meant a good combination of socialism and capitalism. This principle of "Middle-way—Mixed Economy" came into being and Economic Programme Committee Report was submitted on January 25, 1948 which recommended for the appointment of Planning Commission.

Explaining the role played by various system in different periods of history Nehru said, the strongest urge in the world today is that of social justice and equality.[32]

C. Nehru's Ideas on Agriculture and Land Reform

The ideas of Nehru on agricultural development and land reform is very significant. According to him India has been mostly concerned with the rural economic for more than thousand years. It has considered agriculture, animal husbandry, trade and cottage industries as the four pillars of rural economic. Generally, India is known as a country of villages. All these four pillers have been continuously and strongly emphasising in Indian Epic like, Bhagwed Gita, Ramayana, Mahabharat or Puranas. He rightly stated, "Truely speaking, agriculture is not merely an occupation or a business of proposition for the people, it is a tradition, a way of life which for centuries has shaped their thought outlook and culture."[33]

To him, agriculture is the mother of all industries and the maintainer of human life. He further observed that we in India may progress in the domains of science and industry, an undoubtedly we will, the basic fact remains that agriculture in of primary significance to our country and to the world.

For Indian Economy, agriculture is by far the most significant sector. A slight increase in agriculture output has a direct impact on per capita income. To quote him.

"I go on repeating this because agriculture is of the utmost importance. At the present moment, whichever way you start in India you come back to agriculture."[34]

Afterall, food is all a primary necessity. Agriculture, according to Nehru, provides food for all the people and cattle inhabiting in the country. We must become self sufficient in food and not be dependent on other countries for our most essential requirements.[35]

According to Nehru, "agriculture was more important than industry", on December 8, 1963 in his inaugural speech he delivered, "Agriculture is more important than anything else, not excluding big plants, because agricultural production sets the tone to all economic progress. It is agriculture that gives you the where withal for progress. If we fail in agriculture, then we fail in industry also. Agriculture is more important than industry for the simple reason that industry depends on agriculture"

To him, agricultural production is a most vital thing because it provides enough food and raw materials for industry. As such, we must not only have food, but also surplus foods among the major things agriculture is highly important. A hungry is a bad material. Without food it is quite difficult to fight both on domestic front and on the battle front. How can a country fight when it is lacking in food?

According to Nehru agriculture also provides large proportion of India's export. Tea, raw jute, raw-cotton, paper, tobacco, cardamoms, oilseeds, fruits, vegetables, lac, gums and resins, etc. are the main agricultural commodities that earn foreign exchange. Jawaharlal Nehru intended raising the target of agricultural production not only because he wanted adequate supply of food in this country, but because he wanted more food or other agricultural production even for export to fill up the gap in other sectors of the economy of the country. It was only due to the fact that agriculture supplies raw materials for the major industries of the country such as cotton and jute textiles, sugar, edible oils, leather goods etc.

He argued that industry comes after the success of

agriculture. It has became of the utmost importance that agriculture should flourish and should produce the goods and surpluses needed for industries growth. To him, it is agriculture that gives wherewithal for progress. There can be no really stable economy without a stable agricultural basis.

He argued that "Everything else can wait, but not agriculture'. This is true even today. On the biginning of new millennium, the challenges before us is to sustain food security and have some surplus for exports to take advantage of the wind of globalisation, keeping in view of environmental conservation and conservation of natural resources. The Green Revolution can't therefore, be considered to be 100 per cent success. Time has reached to take serious action to decrease the ill-effects of green revolution. Simultaneous efforts need to be made to promote a more sustainable form of agricultural and identify sources for future spurt in agricultural productivity.

If our agricultural foundation is not strong then the industry we seek to build will not have a strong basis. Agriculture, according to him is more important than industry which depends on agriculture. Industry can not develop unless agriculture is sound and stable and progressive.[36] Industrial development, without agricultural development, is quite impossible. Thus, primary attention should be given to agriculture and food which is essential. Moreover, agriculture is bound to continue to be our principal activity.

Nehru on Land Reform

According to Nehru the fundamental issue in our rural economy is how to overhaul the out-dated land tenure system. Socialism in India is irrelevant unless the life of primary producer is made economically better and socially secure. The solution of the problem of upliftment does not merely lie in extending irrigations works or building huge multipurpose projects, but it can be possible more through the land reform in India. The fundamental issue in our rural economy is how to overhaul the out dated land tenure system, because feudalism in any shape or form is a society in hindrance to development and will have to go. Consequently, a number of countries had very big landlords but they have been removed and the land given to the 'Kissans'. He was of the opinion that every farmer should own as much land as he and his family are able to cultivate.[37] The 'Green Revolution' has taken place is one form or the other, in every advanced country. This is important because land or the agrarian problem is the biggest problem of Asia.[38] It is only due to fact that all other problems sink into insignificance before it. As a Chairman of the National Planning Commission appointed by the Indian National Congress in 1938 Pt. Nehru had laid down the general principles which would govern land policy in India after British had withdrawn.

"Agricultural land, mines, quarries, rivers and forests are forms of national wealth, ownership of which must rest absolutely in the people of India collectively."

On Zamindars

He stated to Zamindars that their security ultimately lies in a stable economic system and not in the law courts or in any thing else. If there is no peace between them and the vast agrarian population they have no security. If the Zamindars refuse to see beyond this, there will be a revolutionary situation. Hence, we have to consider the reality and put an end to the Zamindar system, reform our land system make it progressive and modernize it.[39]

According to Nehru feudalism was already out of date. The essence of this system had been the shameless exploitation of the peasantry. There had been forced labour, unpaid work all manner of special dues and payments the lords and this lord himself was a India.

On Division of Land

Nehru believed that Zamindars were middlemen who stood between the cultivator and the state. The cultivators are their tenant who pay them rent, a kind of tax for the use of land owned by Zamindars. Zamindars pay a portron as land revenue to the state. To Nehru, land was divided up into three parts:

(i) part one goes to Zamindars

(ii) part two goes to the State

(iii) remaining part remains with the tenent cultivator.

Moreover, all these parts never equal to each other. In this system, cultivators work on the land, it is due to their labour ploughing and sewing and dozens of other activities, that the land produces anything. Consequently, cultivator is obviously entitled to the fruits of the soil.

According to Nehru as a representating society as a whole, state has important functions to perform in the interest of every citizen. While elaborating this point he said, if the government is ours, the state will responsible to the people and its expenditure is also for the benefit of the people. The national revenue will increase, and this will enable the government to do more for the welfare of the 'Kisan'. Canals could be drugs, wells could be constructed, hospitals and dispensaries could be opened in the villages.[40]

As regards Zamindars, he just takes a big share in produce his rent without helping in anyway in the work of production. He thus, becomes a fifth wheel in the coach not only unnecessary but an actual encumbrance, a burden on the law.[41]

In his view, it would take hold of the poorest peasant, the lowliest of all our people whose entire produce went to his landlord and who hardly had enough food to eat. This poor man was kicked and cuffed by everybody, by his landlord, by his landlord's agent, by the police, by the money lenders.[42]

Whatever money was paid to the landlords does not benefit anyone neither the Kisans nor the general public.

Objectives of Land Reform

Nehru classified the objectives of land reform in two way:

(a) increase in agricultural production, and

(b) better distribution of land.

He was well convinced that unless the peasant has a great security of tenure and unless peasant proprietorship is established more widely, there would not be any adequate incentive for higher production. Thus, tiller of land may be secured in the possession of the land which he cultivates.[43] From distribution angle he felt that strongest urge in the world today was that of social justice and equality. The peasants were not only hungry for food but were also hungry for land. Under the feudal system the Zamindars or nobles were landlords of the land, and to them went a great part of the income from it.

He, subsequently advocated the adoption of Japanese farm model consisted of small farms and small farmers which does not permit reduction of workers but at the same time produce more. According to him mechanization of agriculture can be divided into two parts.[44]

(i) one using better tools, better ploughs, better which reduce labour and produce more but not displace human labour.

(ii) on the other hand, if we use big machines for the mechanisation of agriculture they displace human labour and when human labour has nothing to do, it creates social problems without increasing production.

He was of the view that land reforms had a peculiar significance because without them more especially in highly congested country like India, there could be no radical improvement in productivity in agriculture. He considered it moving and changing, something, revolutionary. It may well change the face of India. We must not, therefore, consider these problems in narrow, legalistic and juristic sense.[45] He considered it scientific impersonal and he had nothing to do with his love for the Zamindars or the tenant. Regarding fixation of land revenue, rent or land-tax he was of the opinion that no taxation or rent in justified of the income is below this limit. Thus, he advocated for radical changes in land laws for real relief and provide social justice and increase agricultural produce.

D. Nehru's Ideas on Cottage and Small Scale Industries and Rural Industrialisation

Nehru defined the term cottage industry or home industry as the artisans or craftsman usually worked in their houses or in small group.[46] According to him its chief characteristics were as follows:

(i) the master craftmen took apprentices and taught them their crafts.

(ii) weavers have their own looms, spinners their own spinning wheels.

(iii) spinning is quite widespreed and in the spare time industry of girls and women.

(iv) sometimes there are small factories where a number of looms are collected and the weavers work together.

(v) each weaver work separately at his own loom and there is really no difference between his working at home or at some other place in company with other weavers and their looms. The samll factory is wholly unlike the modern factory with its big machinery".[47]

Importance

To him, this type of cottage industries flourished all over the world. In India these industries were very advanced. But he made it clear that new mechanical inventions made a great deal of difference to cottage and small industries all over the world. The old "Self sufficient village economy" in India had long ceased to exist. Because of state policies auxiliary cottage industries had died off and because largely they could not complete with rising machine industry. Ill equipped an almost unawarded, the over-burdened village was thrown into the world market was tossed about hitter and thither. It could not complete on even terms.[48] The rural industries play important role in the national economy of the country. The economic condition of the peasants is most deplorable, their standard of living is very low, they are indebted and suffering from chronic under employment and unemployment. Nehru rightly stated "The importance of village industries and more especially Khadi requires no profit today".[49] To him, whatever advance industrialisation on a big machine may be made in our country the growth of village and small industries is highly essential to tackle the vast and chronic problem of unemployment and under employment and to produce a balanced economy for the nation. The solution of poerty, unemployment and regional imbalances lies in the widespread growth of village industries in a poor and over-populated country like ours. He advocated for these industries. He further observed that our objective was not only to increase production by utilising the wasted man-power of India as well as the wasted time of a large number of people, but also create self-reliance among the masses.

As per his opinion, the vast growing population of India

cannot be industrialised in sufficient number within any reasonable time. Large numbers remain poor and unemployed. Heavy industries do not solve the problems of millions in India consequently, we have to develop the village and cottage industry in a big way. The development of 'Khadi and Village Industries'[50] in our country is of paramount significance to the solution of unemployment and to advancement of economy as a whole for him, the welfare state has no meaning unless every individual is employed and take part in national building activities.[51]

Infrastructure

It is better to find employed for large numbers of people at a low income level than to keep most of them unemployed.[52] Poverty of India can't be removed without development of cottage and small-scale industries.

Moreover, Jawaharlal Nehru strongly stressed on the development electric power, machine-making, ship-building, chemicals, locomotives, automobiles, wealth-producing and work producing industries he also emphasised simultaneously on the development of cottage and small scale industries. Consequent up on this, the significance of village industries, house-hold industries, cottage industry and small industry is great.[53]

As a remedial measure to him, this can be balanced in cottage industries in which time gap is not large. Thus, in planning we have to balance heavy industry, light industry, village industry and cottage industry to prevent the gap between the pumping in of money and production. His objectives aimed at maximum production, equitable distribution and full employment. But according to him with India's vast and growing population, this can't be achieved by having big industry only or cottage industry only. We have to ensure that wealth is not accumulated in the hands of a few but is distributed equally. His ideas of cottage and small-scale industries was a decentralised one. He was not in favour of concentration of industries in few selected areas or regions, except in few cases. He wanted it to be dispersed all over the country, specially in rural areas so that the villagers were not compelled to leave their home villages.[54]

Evils

According to him, there are not only economic but also psychological reasons that is why we should pay special attention towards the proper development of cottage and small-scale industries. The development cottage industry will not only bring about economic upliftment of the villager but it will also bring about a Psychological change in him as much as it will satisfy his creative instinct. Nehru advocated use of modern technology with precautions. The latest scientific techniques should be taken advantage of but in doing so one must remember what is feasible and available to the villager. If power is very cheap and easily available in the villages, it should be taken full advantage of it. If the latest type of cottage machines are too expensive, or can't be easily available and repaired in the villages, it is not useful to the villagers under present circumstances.

Thus, we shall never be able to move the India of the rural masses through mere multiplication of big factories. It can only be reached through Khadi and Village Industries. Furthermore, village industries are quite necessary.

E. Nehru on Khadi Industries

It is now agreed on all hands and fronts that in order to provide sizable employment to the people and at the same time produce a large number of consumer goods, it is essential to spread a net work of small, village, cottage industries and Khadi industry throughout the country-side in such a manner that the rural population is able to organise industrial activities side by side with agricultural work.[55]

Importance

According to Nehru today, Khadi is essential to make India more self-sufficient in the matter of cloth. He wanted to reduce dependence on foreign cloths, and achieve self reliance through khadi. He advocated that the necessity of Khadi is even greater in case of war or crisis when automatically foreign imports will cease. It will supply the growing demand, will force mill owners to keep their prices down. So even from the point of view of war emergency khadi is necessary.[56]

It was a false notion that khadi can't be manufactured on a large scale. Khadi organisation has to capacity in it to spread out at short notice.

According to him, as mentioned in his, 'Glimpses of World History' the cloth we wear in khadi is a hand spun and hand woven, and is thus entirely a product of the cottages and mud-huts of India.[57] Khadi tried with some success to bridge the gap between the city and the village. It brought nearer to each other, the middle class intelligent and the peasantry. Khadi clothing has a marked psychological effect on the weavers as well as the beholders. The lower middle class no longer tried to ape the richer class in the matter of clothes or feel humiliated in the cheaper atire. They feel indeed not only dignified but a little superior to those who still flaunt silks and satins. Even the poorers feel something of this dignity and self respect.

He was of the opinion that spinning wheel was not to be the rival of machinery. It was to be kind of secondary occupation, an auxiliary industry. Spinning was also to be a partial stand by for the vast numbers of un-employed who had nothing to do and who are such a burden on the land.Nehru stated that Kisan can easily spin threads on charkha and grow a little cotton on land. The village carpenter can make the charkha at low cost and everyone can easily learn to handle them. Unemployment can be rooted out at once if all kisan women of their house holds start spinning. In this way they can also get more cloth for the needs. Consequently, many caders, weavers, dyers and washermen would secure employment. The country's wealth can increase and their basic troubles would end. Thus, he was of the view that khadi was the way to find work for these men. Khadi is the sheer, solid economic position. If Charkha found favour many of our country men can find employment once more and we had to eredicate poverty we must first do away with that wide spread unemployment.[58] Pt. Nehru wanted khadi industry should be developed on modern productive technology. To him, Gandhi had tried with some success to improve the charkha and the takli and increase their productive capacities. He believed that khadi had a definite political, social and economic values and as such it must be encouraged.[59] This movements and charkha spinning wheel were not meant to compete with the big machines. It was wrong to believe that it would compete the large industries. He actually desired to establish co-ordination between the two. Let the big manufacturer, each in his own place and within his respective legitimate sphere. There was no inherent conflict between the two ways of production and there meed be none. He, thus stress for its revolutionary character. It could become a force in society if we develop its economic character. It was his support for khadi industry that he had constituted permanent khadi commission with adequate funds for its development and improvement. He however recognised the fact also that it must develop under the impetus of its own strength and not cling too much to help for Government.

F. Nehru on Community Development

He observed that India consists very largely of villages; our activities must also largely be rural to reach the village so that we may work with and for the masses. The problem of our country can't be solved without solving the problems of villages. He made it clear that the community projects and the National Extension Schemes were both meant for the rural areas. He stated, "I think that they are probably the most revolutionary thing that is happening in India these days."[60]

Importance

To him, community development is both a technique as well as a movement. It remains as a technique when it is concerned with only a section of agricultural population or covers only some of their problems. But when it embraces within its wide arms are millions of rural men, women and communities alongwith the totality of their numerous problems, as in Nehru's India, it gets universalised. It becomes a revolutionary movement, as he observed.

"These community projects and National Extension Service Scheme have, I think, created a revolutionary atmosphere in our country side."[61] According to him, the whole project behind the community development and Panchayati Raj was to create opportunities for human beings to grow, to be able to think, to be able to act, to be able to co-operate with each other and act together.[62]

Our Community Development Schemes represent a rural reconstruction programme which promises to transform the country side and the vast population that live there. Thus for, these community projects have aimed at what might be called amenities, like roads, tanks, wells, school building and so on. Our community Development Schemes represent a rural reconstruction programme which promises to transform the country side and the vast population that live there. He believed that agricultural production will certainly increase rapidly under community Development Projects. He was in favour of extending these projects to Punchayati Raj. He had welcomed the co-ordination of the activities of the Social Welfare Board with Community Development Movement because both covers the whole country and both have fundamentally the some objectives. It would be unfortunate of these two agencies pulled is different direction or worked independently of each other. Thus, their activities must be closely co-ordinated. He introduced Community Development Schemes and National Extension Services at the National level. In his words, "I see the Community Project and National Extension Service spread in our rural areas with a speed which is remarkable and without precedent in history. That is the great revolution that is taking place in the village, and in the heart of India".

This was his unique idea which had been applied in rural economy. In his opinion, these community schemes are not a replica or a copy of something from abroad, although we have learnt most from other countries. There are essentially on Indian growth.

Emphasis in our Community Development Programme on self-help and co-operation, are meant to provide opportunities to the rural section for the full play of their talent energies and intellects in cause of improving rural conditions including social economic transformation of village life. After all, the main aim of Community Development and Panchayati Raj was to develop this outlook and a spirit of self-reliance amongst the people. Since the rural people are perfectly untrained in most of the rural areas Nehru suggested for the provision of proper training to these people to give them the chance of shouldering responsibility and learning by their own mistakes.[63]

Moreover, the accent of the Community Development is definitely on the action by the rural community itself. 'Self-help is the best help' Communities rise by their own doings. Self-help and self-reliance are crucial to the success of community development method.

For him, it was necessary to plan to direct, to organise and to co-ordinate and to create conditions in which spontaneous growth from below is possible.

Furthermore, no improvements will be lasting unless the villager himself comes to understand and feel the want of them.

Hence, it becomes imperative that a bold step be taken whereby more and more responsibility could be transferred to the people. The people were not merely to be consulted but effective powers was to be entrusted to them.

Nehru's Socialistic Pattern of society was a totality of economic and social objectives. Provision of economic adequacy and promotion of social justice constitute its two main strands. In other words reduction in regional disparities and promotion of balanced development an between different locations are crucial to the concept of 'socialistic pattern of society'. Removal of inequalities in income and opportunities on between rural and urban localities is thus, an avowed mission of this 'Socialistic pattern of society'.[64]

Furthermore, Jawaharlal Nehru had felt that from the point of view of balanced development, we have to lay greater stress on many small industries in our villages, make them slightly urbanized, lessen the gap between them and urban areas and increase the facilities available to the people who live there, instead of concentrating on the towns and cities and drawing out people from the villages and thus creating problems in the cities. After all, cities are moving and they will go ahead. But the villages require very great attention. According to him country is committed to a socialistic pattern of society and as such no action can succeed unless there is local strength to carry it on.[65]

G. Nehru on Co-operative Principles

Nehru was a very firm believer in the co-operative principles. He believed in it so much that he would like to introduce it in all the departments of state, including the whole structure of government. He would like to have a cooperataive common wealth and even he wished to extend it on an international scale.[66] So far as India is concerned he felt that a co-operative should be formed so that people of the village should know each other. The co-operative should encourage cohesion and coming together of village people. In his view, village should be like a large family, while the Panchayat would represent the administrative aspect of village life; the co-operation will represent the "economic side of village life."[67]

Nehru was of the view that as civilization advances and society becomes more and more complex, the element of co-operative endeavour becomes more important. By working together they could produce for more food and other necessaries than by working singly.[68] It is evident from his writings that on gready and grasping capitation grew, a cleek to it was devised by the advanced people in the co-operative movement. Co-operative institutions must occupy the commanding heights of the economy on behalf of the community.[69] In other words, the co-operative way is based on mutual co-operation. This method is the best method of bringing about a social and economic reconstruction of our country specially in the rural areas. It is a form of economic organisation in which it is possible to achieve maximum harmoney between individual initiative and freedom and social obligation. In the co-operative sphere, there would be sufficient scope for private entrepreneurs to earn reasonable profits on a continuing basis but they should be content with a lower margin of financial gains consistent with community interest. It is only through co-operative method that the social and economic justice can be secured.[70] Co-operation avoids the evils of capitalism and socialism and ensure advantage of both. It will level up the poorer section of the community economically and socially.[71]

According to Nehru, in the past the co-operatives had been chiefly societies for credit purposes which removed the money lenders and middle men. But he wanted the co-operatives to perform many other services. The peasant in India is very weak. He can make good only if he joins others through a co-operative. By forming co-operatives the peasants can pool their resources for providing credit and for getting supplies of seeds, fertilizers etc. and can organise to scale their products. If it functions properly, they will help in introducing cottage and small industries and other auxiliary activities in the villages.

In his opinion, co-operative movement has an enormous future provided it must think of mass needs and try to meet then "Where there is good will and co-operation there is an abundance and variety of wealth".[72] To him, the work we are doing in India is extraordinarily exciting and fascinating. It has an element of creativeness and artistry in it. Even in Soviet Russia" Owner producer co-operataives" have played on important part in industrial growth.

Co-operative Farming and Nehru

A good deal of literature has been produced in India to highlight the theoretical flows as well as the practical merits and demerits of co-operative farming. Nehru personally did much to arouse the enthusiasm of the peasant and cultivator not only for a more equitable system of land tenure but also better methods of production and distribution.[73] In its Nagpur session, Indian National Congress under the leadership of Pt. Nehru adopted a resolution a programme of co-operative farming in India in 1959. Co-operative farming refers to a system of agricultural organisation wherein cultivators of an area voluntarily associate together, pool their individual land holdings for purposes of cultivation and manage the whole farm as one unit under an elected management. The individual ownership of land is however, retained. In other words, co-operative farming essentially is a system wherein there is individual ownership and joint management of land.

It is obvious that its main objective is to combine the incentive of ownership with the large scale public enterprise possible in agriculture. To quote him, "Any radical change in the land system involving large scale co-operative and collective farming, must be preceded or accompained by the ending of present Zamindar or landlord system wherever it prevails.[74] Large scale state and collective or co-operative farms must be established. But it can be done only after removal of rested can be done only after removal of vested interests. The co-operative farming is a desirable mode of organising agriculture. There is also need for creating a true understanding of the operation of co-operative farms on the part of middle and large peasants and small peasants who constitute about 60 per cent of cultivating families so that they may not see in this mode of farming a danger to their own individual organisation and may cease to oppose what is essentially right and very important.

The agrarian revolution, as such, over which Nehru presided was to a large relent a revolution by consent or conversion not by compulsion. He never liked monopolies or concentration of power. In other words, the normal tendency should be far decentralization of all kinds of power so that people may equally share them.[75]

For Nehru, co-operative farming is not necessarily a concentration of power. It is spread out.[76] Together with co-operative and collective farming a progressive industrialization of the country is highly desirable in order to raise the standard of living and provide employment for the unemployment masses.[77]

H. New Economic Reform and Globalisation and Nehru

Material advance without spiritual balance can be disastrous. According to Nehru new vistas are daily opening up before man, leading to unthought of promises and potentialities. The phenomenal development of science and technology, if not properly utilised by the nation in the right spirit, may lead to compete annihilation. Consequently, Jawaharlal Nehru observed that the world required to develop a new dimension of mind, new economic order to tackle the various problems arising from the tremendous scientific and technological advancement which had tremendous effects on our economy and called industrial Revolution.[79]

He further stated that technology has made such a great progress today the people tend to forget other things and culture. A kind of technological culture, of course, progress which is good in so far as it goes provided it is balanced by other forms of culture. He observed that it will not profit a man very much if he is clever with his hands or even with his tongue or brain, but has no foundation of character or wide vision. In the absence of these ethical qualities, a society will ultimately perish. So this drift to technology which is inevitable today in the world and in India has to be balanced by the other aspects of culture.

According to Nehru, all this scientific and technological progress in the world is likely to lead to distruction, unless it is balanced by some kind of moral standard and ethical value. When the human material in any country detenorates, it is a matter of great danger.[80]

He observed "while on the one side we see tremendous advance, on the other we notice a disintegration of society, because the cement of moral and ethical standards and patterns of behaviour gradually melts away."[81] In only event, we can't stop or reverse the current of change which science and technology have brought about in great parts of the world. According to him, there is the religious approach which has unfortunately narrowed down to dogmas and ceremonials. The form or shell of religion remains, while the spirit is lost. We can't be untrue to science, because that represents the basic fact of life today.

He was of the view that in our efforts to ensure the material prosperity of the country we have not paid any attention to the spiritual element in human nature. In order to give the individual and the nature a sense of purpose, something to live for and if necessary to die for, we have to revive some philosophy of life and give in the wider sense of the world, a spiritual background to our thinking.[82] We should not forget the basic human element, the ethical and spiritual aspects of life which are ultimately the basis of our culture and civilization and have given some meaning to life.[83]

It does not mean that we attach no significance to other aspects of human life. We do not forget the human factor. We are not merely ought to get more money and more production. We ultimately want better human beings. We want our people to have greater opportunities, not only from an economic or material point of view but at other levels also.

For Nehru, "material progress can't go far or last long unless it has its foundations in moral principles and high ideas.

While these material achievements are very great, some how we appear to be slipping away from the very essence of utility, culture and civilization rest in the mind and behaviour of man and not in the material evidence of it that we see around us.

His emphasis on ethical and spiritual solution is not unconscious. It is deliberate, quite deliberate. There are good reasons for it.

Liberaliation, privatisation and globalisation are the three pillars on which the edifice of new economic policy has been created in India since 1991. This new economic measure can also be co-related with the ideas of Nehru. Established on

1st January 1995. The World Trade Organisation (WTO) a successor of GATT (1947) in the embodiment of the results of Uruguay Round (UR) held during 1986-93. The various agreements reached in the important sectors and commitments made by memberss now 141, reflect clearly a keen desire on their part to establish and strengthen overtime a multilateral trading system at the global level, based on 'rural rather than power' which is equitable free, fair and nondiscriminatory. However, there have emerged serious distortions and asymmetrics in the functioning of world trading order and monetry system due to variety of causes since 1956 and also after 1995 which if not corrected, will jeopardise their smooth running and have serious reprecussions for the prosperity and sustainable development of both North and South. No serious attempt has been made till today by the industrialised countries to minimise these inequalities which in fact, have shown an increasing trend.

I. Nehru on Capital Formation

After independence, the problem of economic development, particularly of industrial development was faced by Nehru. He adopted the device of planned economic development. In normal course, Nehru wanted to finance, economic development schemes through taxation, internal public debt and deficit financing.

Jawaharlal Nehru did not like to practice deficit financing in respect of under developed economy beyond cε rtain limits.

Internal public debt and taxation are closely connected with the saving capacity of both public and private. For Nehru public savings means taxation and other forms of compulsory savings.[84] The nations's economic growth is no simple matter. He had to plan the nation's savings and long term investment with great care. According to him, in order to progress, we must save money for progress, every year whether we are a communist state or a socialist or capitalist state.[85]

He was convinced that growth of capital for investment depends on the value of savings. In turn, saving depends on the level of money income to the people and on a number of other factors i.e. prospensity to save on the part of individuals as well as private and public undertakings. The higher the incomes the larger would be the volume of savings in the country. If incomes are so low that nothing remains after meeting the base needs of life, the volume of savings must necessarily be small. This is the case with the under-developed or poor countries of the world.[86]

Process of Capital Formation and Nehru

To him the process of capital formation involves three distinct, it inner-dependent stages:

1. The stage of saving
2. The stage of canalization or mobilization of savings, and
3. The stage of investment

In the first stage resources which might be used for current consumption are set aside and so become available for other purposes. In the second stage resources are assembled from among those released by domestic saving and then placed in the hands of investors and in the third and final stage the resources are actually committed to the production of capital goods.

The first stage, stage of savings according to Nehru plays most important role in the process of capital formation.

(i) As the per capita income grows, the level of savings increases more than proportionately and

(ii) As the level of savings increases the rate of capital formation also increases leading to a rise in the rate of economic growth.

The second, stage of mabilization of saving is also very useful for capital formation. The activity of saving is widely deffused throughout the community and carried on by the persons who generally lack the skill and personal characteristics for active investment. Once, when savings have been mobilized, they are made available to the business who invest them which is the final stage of capital formation.

Investment raises the productive capacity of the economy and should, in normal circumstances, lead to an increase in the total production of the economy. However, because of a lack of investment opportunities in the developing countries, a large parts of savings are utilized for speculative purposes which do not add to the productive capacity of the economy. The lack of investment opportunities in the developing countries arises due to small domestic markets, incapable of supporting the scale of modern establishments. Transportation facilities and power are lacking on expensive, the price of capital equipment is high and skilled workers, technicians, and managers are scarce.

Sources of Capital

Nehru advocated two type of sources of capital:

(i) Domestic

(ii) Foreing

The level of savings as he stated in the developing countries is very low. In these countries productive investment is not small because there is no surplus, it is small because the surplus is used to maintain unproductive hoards of retainers, and to build pyramids, temples and other durable consumer goods, instead to create productive capital. If this surplus were going instead as profits to capitalists, or as taxes to productivity inclined government, much higher levels of investment would be possible without inflation.

J. Nehru on Human Resource Development

According to Nehru the rate of our economic growth obviously depends on the growth of population. There is a big pressure of rapidly growing population which consumes whatever greater production is made, leaving little room for savings or investment for further advance.[87] Thus, the basic problem before Nehru became one of how is an under-developed and poverty striken country like India, surpluses could be created for investment and greater production. In his opinion, that percentage is always a small percentage in developing economies and big in developed one.[88]

The worst thing about poverty is that it implies a vicious circle of poverty. In under developed countries there are commulative forces at work which make the poor poorer.[89] It implies a circular constellation of forces tending to act and react upon one another in such a way as to keep a poor country in a state of poverty. Being poor, a man lacks the means to prosper and since he lacks the means to prosper, he must remain poor. The vicious circle is complete. Poverty leads to inefficiency and incapacity to do well, and inefficiency and incapacity must end in poverty.

The rate of saving and investment in under developed countries is too low to make for rapid development and since, the rate of savings and investment are too small. It must remain under developed. Hence, country is poor because is poor.[90] But now, it is the ambition of all under developed countries to treat the road of accelerated economic development or self-reliance[91] or self growth.[92] Thus, for rapid economic development somehow how means must be created for economic growth, the rate of savings must be raised and investment must be encouraged by all possible means. Nehru was of the view that coercive methods could be employed.

K. Pattern of Taxation and Nehru

Nehru was of the view that there is a limit to our capacity

to do things and there is a limit to taxation. We can't go beyond that without disturbing the whole structure of our economy.

Since, he was the perfect advocate of socialist pattern of society which requires a well-knit fiscal policy which can play a significant role in raising required resources of state.[93] Primarily taxation attempts to reduce the volume of income with higher income groups and transfer the income to the Public authorities who may use revenue to raise the standard of living of the poor. He was of the view that "to give to the poor and depressed." We must take from the "rich and those who possess."[94]

He was very categorical on direct and indirect taxation. According to him, one of the principal objects of taxation, apart from that of running the government machine, is to equalise income. To prevent disparity is the social object of taxation. To him, income and wealth are the main factors responsible for present inequalities in the society. The whole object of a graded income-tax and super tax is to lessen the big differences that exist.[95] He wanted that direct taxes should be progressive. He stated, "Taxation should be direct and as far as possible indirect taxation should be abolished. Further, this direct taxation should be steeply graduated so as to fall mainly on the larger income".[96]

He further observed, "all manner of heavy taxes, which are in the nature of confiscation swallow up individual property rights for the public good" under Nehru's socialistic pattern of taxation the whole meaning of taxation changes. The burden of taxation does not fall on the shoulders of the common strata of society. The tax system aims at to collect the part of the surplus product as a part of revenue. He, as such, wanted to equalise the present distinction of wealth and maintain principles of taxation. The burden of taxation must be increased on the rich and decreased and even removed entirely from the poor. As regard land-revenue/land rent he was of the firm opinion that the very poor holders of land should be entirely exempted from taxation[97] so that taxation must play a vital role in bringing about equality in the distribution of wealth by levelling down the wealth of the rich.[98]

In Nehru's scheme of socialistic pattern of society taxation indirect taxation particularly states sales tax, state excise duty had no place as these taxes are not based on progressive principle of taxation.

L. Nehru on Stages of Economic Growth

According to the Nehru, we in India are struggling to get out of the morass of poverty and to reach the stage of what is called the take-off into sustained economic growth. We want to cross the barrier of poverty and reach the stage where growth becomes relatively spontaneous. The under developed country is on this side of the barrier.[99] In his opinion, India is an under-developed country considering its vast potential. In short its economy is gaining an element of dynamism which is a preduce to the next stage of self-growth.[100]

Ever since the Industrial Revolution economists and historians have made it a fasinating part time of dividing the evolution of an economic growth into a few distinct stages of growth by fixing their attention on some key variable. As every body knows that human civilization has been divided, into stone age, iron age, bronze age, and atomic age depending upon the tools of production used or methods to produce the means of living.[101] Nehru in his Glimpses of world history has discussed following stages of an individual beginning at the bottom.

1. Savage
2. Nomadic stage of society:

3. Stage in which man lived on the fruits of the virgin earth rising to the pre tribal postoral stage.
4. Socially organised agricultural stage in which people take on active part in economic production by telling the soil and sowing crop.

These methods to produce the means of living according to Nehru, were the most important thing in man's life and society's life in every stage. They dominated each period of history and influenced all activities and social relation of that period.[102]

Nehru was a opinion that methods of production at a certain period of economic history correspond to a definite stage in the growth of the people.[103] According to this view, as the methods of production change the economic structure changes and this is followed by a change in people's idea, law, politics etc.

About traditional society it was fact that there was an upper limit to the level of attainable percapital output due to absence of modern science and technology. Man was a creature of the circumstances with little capability to manipulate his environment to his economic advantage. In his own words, "you simply can't leap or skip our different stages but you have to grow from one into another.[104]

Furthermore, a take-off stage can't take place at the very commencement of economic development in a stagnant economy India's economy had been almost stagnant for a long period at the period when we began planning. Regarding stagnant economy he stated, "A stagnant economy gets stuck in the routes and it is difficult to get a more on. Once it gets into motion it is easier to go on as greater speed."[105]

Nehru defined take-off stages as "a self-feeding, self-propelling, self-developing economy."[106]

Take-off stage or self-reliance may be distinguished from

self-sufficiency, which means that the country produces all that it needs and it has to import nothing of goods and services from foreign countries. A country gets moving only when it has started this process of self-growth. Only the hard work and the determination of the people of under developed economics themselves can produce the solution to their problem.

M. Nehru on Population Planning

According to Jawaharlal Nehru what is important is that each person should produce.[107] We want a society in which every body is a producer is some way or the other. "Since, everyone is a consumer he must be a producer also."[108] The man power planning is utmost importance. It means, the balancing of the demand and supply of labour power in various occupation. Economic development is intended for the welfare and well being of the people of the country concerned. When population increase labour, one of the basic factors, also increases consequently, production also increases. The growth of population affects economic developments and vice-versa.

Nehru, like emient economists, C. Clark, E. Hegan and Max. holds the view that a great deal has been said and written about our tremendous population how it overwhelms us and how we cannot solve any problem till the Indian population is checked. Nehru had no desire for the Indian population to go on increasing.

However, Nehru declared, "if we increase our production, agriculture and other, and if the population is put to work for production then we are not over-populated".

For Nehru, fast growing population reduces country's capacity to save and invest. Pressure of rapidly growing population which consumed whatever greater production is made leaving little room for saving and investment for further development. Consequently, country is caught up by vicious circle that is its

Low Saving →| Low Investment →| Low Income →| Low Saving

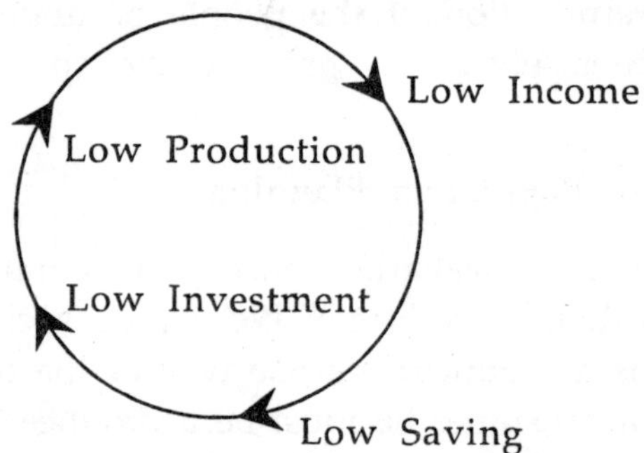

According to him, "The main problem in the poor and under-developed economy is low surplus could be created for investment and greater production. He accepted the food problem as acute for production, people live on starvation line, they are ill-fed, ill-clothed ill-doctored, ill-housed, ill-educated and sleeped in poverty. Nehru had accepted it. We in India have been trying to tackle this problem as best as we could "I confess that we have not succeeded remarkably and the growth of population in this big country is rather alarming".[109]

As population grows, it rather overhelms the efforts we make towards economic growth. He mightly observed.

"We have thus, to face a kind of race between the rate of economic growth and the rate at which population grows".[110] Consequent upon this, a seriöus threat of food problem comes out. Population problem creates all kinds of social conflicts, and ultimately political conflicts and the like. To him dealing with economic advance, social advance or population problem is connected with world problem. He had to face dilema as population problem affects us in all our social activities.

The country has gone in for planning for economic and social growth. Economic planning in our country can't be successful without family planning. Population control has now been accepted as an element in the strategy of development to achieve faster rate of economic growth.

To him, raising the level of literacy education, economic and social status play important role in restricting family size.

Although, he was interested in tackling it directly through family planning yet, he was quite certain that the first problem before India, is the problem of poverty. He had been repeatedly laying stress on the need for economic growth. To him, only family planning can't not solve the entire problem. The planning commission and other officials of Government are working for this purpose.

REFERENCES

1. Talks with Nehru, *A Discussion between Jawaharlal Nehru and Normal Cousins*, 1951, p. 22.
2. Nehru, Jawaharlal, *Glimpses of the World History*, Lindsay Drummond, London 1939, p. 527.
3. Sha, A.B., (Ed.) *Jawaharlal Nehru : A Critical Tribute Manaklalas*, Bombay, 1965, p. 51.
4. Nehru, Toynbee and Attlee, Earl C.R., *India and the World*, 1962, p. 38.
5. Nehru Jawaharlal, *An Autobiography, op. cit.*, p. 522.
6. Nehru Jawaharlal, *Speeches of Jawaharlal Nehru*, Vol. I, 1967, p. 125.
7. Nehru Jawaharlal, *Eighteen Months in India*, 1938, p. 14.
8. Nehru Jawaharlal, *India and the World*, 1962, p. 39.
9. Nehru Jawaharlal, *Speeches of Jawaharlal Nehru, op. cit.*, Vol. II, 1967, p. 76.
10. *Ibid*.
11. Nehru Jawaharlal, *Selected Works of Jawaharlal Nehru*, Vol. XI, 1968, p. 327.
12. Nehru Jawaharlal, *Speeches of Jawaharlal Nehru*, Vol. II, 1967, p. 476, op.et.

13. Mishra, O.P., *The Economic Philosophy of Pt. Jawaharlal Nehru:* Chugh Publications, Allahabad, 1978, p. 64.

14. Nehru Jawaharlal, *An Autobiography,* Bodly Head, London, 1936.

15. Nehru Jawaharlal, *Draft Outline of the Third Five Year Plan—A Symposium,* I.C.C. Publication, p. 225.

16. Planning & Development, Government of India, 1956, p. 8.

17. Nehru Jawaharlal, *Speeches of Jawaharlal Nehru, op. cit.,* Vol. II, 1967, p. 45.

18. Nehru Jawaharlal, *The Unity of India,* 1948, p. 117.

19. Nehru Jawaharlal, *Talks of Jawaharlal Nehru with Normal Cousins,* 1951, *op. cit.,* p. 23.

20. Krishnamurti, Y.G., *Jawaharlal Nehru—The Man His Ideas,* Popular Book Depot, Bombay, 1944, p. 21.

21. Nehru Jawaharlal, *Talks with Normal Cousins, op. cit.,* pp. 24-25.

22. Nehru Jawaharlal, *Selected Works of Jawaharlal Nehru,* Vol. VI, 1974, p. 20.

23. Nehru Jawaharlal, *Glimpses of World History,* 1949, *op. cit.,* pp. 353-54.

24. Nehru Jawaharlal, *Ibid.,* 350.

25. Frank Moraes, *Jawaharlal Nehru—A Biography,* Macmillan, New York, 1956, p. 32.

26. Chibber, *Jawaharlal Nehru,* Vikas Publications, Delhi, 1970, p. 40.

27. Rao, V.K.R.V., *The Nehru Legacy,* Popular Prakashan, Bombay, 1971, p. 67.

28. Gopal, Ram, *The Trials of Jawaharlal Nehru,* Book Centre, Delhi, 1962, p. 22.

29. Nehru Jawaharlal, *Selected Works of Jawaharlal Nehru,* Vol. VI, 1974, p. 7.

30. Nehru Jawaharlal, *Glimpses of World History,* 1949, *op. cit.,* p. 559.

31. Nehru Jawaharlal, *The Unity of India, op. cit.,* 1948, p. 117.

32. Nehru Jawaharlal, *India and the World,* 1962, p. 39.

33. Nehru Jawaharlal, *Speeches of Jawaharlal Nehru,* 1967, *op. cit.,* p. 65.

34. Design, P.B., *Planning in India,* 1951-78, Vikas Publising House, New Delhi, p. 19.

35. Michael Brecher, *Nehru: A Political Biography*, 1969, Oxford University Press, London, p. 195.

36. Khare, N.B., *Nehru as I know Him*, Bombay, 1957, p. 47.

37. Nehru Jawaharlal, *Selected Works of Jawaharlal Nehru, op. cit.*, Vol. III, 1972, p. 374.

38. Nehru Jawaharlal, *Speeches of Jawaharlal Nehru*, Vol. II, 1967, p. 407.

39. Sarin, L.N., *Jawaharlal Nehru*, S. Chand and Co., Delhi, 1968, p. 49.

40. Nehru Jawaharlal, *Selected Works of Jawaharlal Nehru*, Vol. III, 1972, p. 374, *op. cit*.

41. Nehru Jawaharlal, *Glimpses of World History*, 1949, p. 424.

42. Nehru Jawaharlal, *Speeches of Jawaharlal Nehru*, Vol. II, 1967, p. 205.

43. Karanja, R.K., *The Philosophy of Mr. Nehru*, Allen & Unwin, London, 1966, p. 67.

44. Nehru Jawaharlal, *Glimpses of World History, op. cit.*, 1949, p. 364.

45. Nehru Jawaharlal, *Selected Work on Jawaharlal Nehru*, Vol. IX, 1976, p. 666, *op. cit*.

46. Nehru Jawaharlal, *Glimpses of World History, op. cit.*, 1949, p. 349.

47. Gopal, S., *Jawaharlal Nehru: A Biography*, Book Centre, Delhi, 1963, p. 51.

48. Nehru Jawaharlal, *Selected Works of Jawaharlal Nehru, op. cit.*, Vol. XII, 1979, p. 547.

49. Nehru Jawaharlal, *Ibid.*, Vol. X, 1979, p. 541.

50. Nehru Jawaharlal, *Speeches of Jawaharlal Nehru, op. cit.*, Vol. II, 1967, pp. 96-97.

51. Nehru Jawaharlal, *Ibid.*, p. 97.

52. Nehru Jawaharlal, *Selected Works on Jawaharlal Nehru*, Vol. XII, 1979, p. 570.
    Note: Allahabad 2 July, 1942 Forward to Nym Wale's China Builds for Democracy (Allahabad, 1942), Reprinted in Asia and the America (New York) January, 1943.

53. Nehru Jawaharlal, *Speeches of Jawaharlal Nehru*, Vol. III, 1970, pp. 51-52.

54. Kamraj K., *The Nehru Legacy*, National Book Club Publication, Delhi 1966.

55. Nehru Jawaharlal, *An Autobiography, op. cit.*, 1962, p. 281.
56. Nehru Jawaharlal, *Ibid.*, Vol. X, 1977.
57. Nehru Jawaharlal, *Glimpses of World History, op. cit.*, 1949, p. 349.
58. Nehru Jawaharlal, *An Autobiography,* 1962, p. 523.
59. Nehru Jawaharlal, *Selected Works of Jawaharlal Nehru, op. cit.*, Vol. II, 1975, p. 238.
60. Nehru Jawaharlal, *Conversation T. Mende,* 1956, p. 111.
61. Nehru Jawaharlal, *Speeches of Jawaharlal Nehru,* Vol. II, 1967, pp. 100-101, *op. cit.*
62. Nehru Jawaharlal, *Ibid.*, Vol. V, 1968, p. 95.
63. Nehru Jawaharlal, *The Discovery of India,* Meridian, Books, London, 1956, p. 448.
64. Karanjia R.K., *Interview with Jawaharlal Nehru,* 1960, pp. 71-72.
65. Nehru Jawaharlal, *Selected Works on Jawaharlal Nehru, op. cit.*, 1973, p. 255.
66. Nehru Jawaharlal, *Selected Works of Jawaharlal Nehru,* Vol. IV, 1973, p. 571, *op. cit.*
67. Nehru Jawaharlal, *Selected Works of Jawaharlal Nehru,* 1964, p. 130.
68. Nehru Jawaharlal, *Glimpses of World History,* 1949, p. 58.
69. Anstey, Vera, *The Economic Development of India,* London, 1952, p. 104.
70. Nehru Jawaharlal, *Selected Works of Jawaharlal Nehru,* Vol. X, 1977, p. 600.
71. Nehru Jawaharlal, *Speeches of Jawaharlal Nehru,* Vol. III, 1970, p. 82.
72. Nehru Jawaharlal, *Selected Works of Jawaharlal Nehru,* Vol. X, 1977, p. 641.
73. Nehru Jawaharlal, *Speeches of Jawaharlal Nehru, op. cit.*, Vol. IV, p. 141.
74. Nehru Jawaharlal, *Selected Works of Jawaharlal Nehru, op. cit.*, Vol. VII, 1975, p. 109.
75. Conversation T. Mende, *op. cit.*, 1956, pp. 46-47.
76. Nehru Jawaharlal, *Selected Works of Jawaharlal Nehru, op. cit.*, Vol. VII, 1975, p. 37.
77. *Interview,* R.K. Karanjia, 1960, p. 103, *op. cit.*

78. Nehru Jawaharlal, *Speeches of Jawaharlal Nehru*, Vol. III, 1970, p. 166.

79. *Interview*, R.K. Karanjia, *op. cit.*, p. 43.

80. Nehru Jawaharlal, *Speeches of Jawaharlal Nehru*, Vol. IV, 1964, p. 169, *op. cit*.

81. Nehru Jawaharlal, *Ibid.*, Vol. III, 1970, p. 426.

82. Nehru Jawaharlal, *Ibid.*, Vol. IV, 1964, p. 121.

83. Nehru Jawaharlal, *Glimpses of World History*, 1949, p. 354.

84. Nehru Jawaharlal, *Ibid.*, pp. 360, 560.

85. Nehru Jawaharlal, *Ibid.*, p. 348.

86. Mishra, S.K. & Puri V.K., *Economic Development*, Himalaya Publication, 1996, pp. 411-42, Bombay.

87. Nehru Jawaharlal, *India and the World*, 1962, p. 16.

88. Nehru Jawaharlal, *Speeches of Jawaharlal Nehru*, Vol. III, 1970, p. 97.

89. Nehru Jawaharlal, *Ibid.*, Vol. IV, 1964, p. 112.

90. Nehru Jawaharlal, *Ibid.*, p. 176.

91. Nehru Jawaharlal, *Ibid.*, p. 88.

92. Nehru Jawaharlal, *Ibid.*, Vol. IV, 1964, p. 112, *op. cit*.

93. Murti, B.S.H., *Nehru Foreign Policy:* The Beacon Information and Publications, New Delhi, p. 16.

94. Nehru Jawaharlal, *Speeches of Jawaharlal Nehru*, Vol. III, 1970, p. 63.

95. Nehru Jawaharlal, *Selected Works of Jawaharlal Nehru, op. cit.*, Vol. IV, 1973, p. 65.

96. Nehru Jawaharlal, *Selected Works of Jawaharlal Nehru, op. cit.*, p. 63.

97. Nehru Jawaharlal, *Selected Works of Jawaharlal Nehru, op. cit.*, p. 259.

98. Dube, R.P., *Jawaharlal Nehru A Study in Ideology and Social Change*.

99. Nehru Jawaharlal, *Speeches of Jawaharlal Nehru*, Vol. IV, 1964, p. 111.

100. Nehru Jawaharlal, *Ibid.*, p. 112.

101. Nehru Jawaharlal, *Glimpses of World History*, 1949, *op. cit.*, p. 544.

102. Venteshwaran, R.J., *The Impact of Jawaharlal Nehru on Indian Economy*, Oxford Book Co., Calcutta, 1962, p. 15.
103. Bakshi, S.R., *Nehru and His Political Ideology*, Criterian Publication, p. 156.
104. *Interview*, R.K. Karanjia, *op. cit.*, 1960, p. 38.
105. Nehru Jawaharlal, *Speeches of Jawaharlal Nehru*, Vol. IV, 1964, p. 142.
106. *Interview*, R.K. Karanjia, 1960, p. 41.
107. Nehru Jawaharlal, *Speeches of Jawaharlal Nehru*, Vol. III, 1970, p. 405.
108. Rao, V.K.R.V., Planning without Dogma, A Study of Nehru, Refique Zakaria; *A Times of India*, Publication, Bombay, 1960, pp. 307-08.
109. Mishra, Girish, *Nehru and the Economic Policies*, Sterling Publishers, pp. 127-28.
110. Moraes, Frank, *Jawaharlal Nehru*: *A Biography*, Jaicos Publishing House, 1959, p. 24.

3

Nehru on Socialism

The impact of socialism on Nehru is overpowering and his adherence to socialistic doctrine was life-long. Nehru wrote, "it is a philosophy of life and of the methods to be adopted to attain a certain end."[1] On socialism he stated, "Socialism is thus, for me not merely an economic doctrine which I favour, it is a vital creed which I hold with all my head and heart[2], because the object of socialism and communism is to bring about a change in human habits, instricts, desires and urges. The whole atmosphere should be changed in that direction."[3]

According to Nehru Scientific socialism can be defined as Marxism socialism as understood in India usually means vague idealism as some body think, demanding justice for the under-dogs. But to Nehru modern socialism is something for more than this, it is called scientific socialism. It interprets history, economics, politics and indeeds all branches of life in terms of certain fundamental laws.[4]

For him, socialism is an economic theory that endeavours to understand and solve the problems that afflict the world today. It is also a way of looking at history and to try to find from its wayward course the law, if any, that govern human society. Vast number of people all over the world believe in it and seek to realise it.[5] Socialism implies the ownership of the means of production and distribution by the society as a whole. The state being the representative of whole society would own control the means of production and distribution collectively and operate them to secure the maximum benefit to the society. It aims at doing away with dangerous disparities in fortunes and providing equal opportunities to all, so that a common level in social and economic progress assured.[6]

Thus, according to Nehru, socialism is of many kinds. Socialism is a vague term which covers many theories but it is needless to enter into them at this stage.

Socialism and Capitalism and Nehru

For Nehru, socialism and capitalism are rival systems or theories is conflict with each other. Socialism is a development, according to him, an inevitable development of capitalism.

It is not so much a question of conflict but a development from one phase to another.[7] He rightly observed "Socialism is an economic doctrine for social organization of the State building which can alone bring salvation to the country."[8] The socialistic theory was that the state, representing society as a whole should own and control the means of production that is land and theories.

According to him, the true civic ideal is the socialist ideal, the communist ideal, which means the common enjoyment of the wealth that is produced in Nehru and by human endeavour.[9] In the words of Nehru,

"But words and labels confuse. What I seek is an elimination of the profit motive in society and its replacement by a spirit of social service, co-operation taking the place of compensation, production for consumption instead of for profit."[10]

Nehru proposed a central Planning authority for running of economic life of the country. The various branches or agencies of production would be developed harmoniously by a central planning authority to serve the best interests of the country as a whole.

Definition

Jawaharlal Nehru had never bothered to find out an appropriate definition of Socialism though, over half a century he remained faithful to socialistic theory. He was careful enough not to define socialism. He himself accepted his inability that "It is not an easy subject for me to write about as I am no expert in it, and as it happens, even the expert and the pandit differ."[11] Then, "I do not see why I should be asked to define socialism in precise, rigid terms."[12]

He thus, expressed that definitions are very difficult, and he did not pressure to define anything because to define any thing, that is big thing, is to limit it.[13] He refrained from giving an appropriate, precise and comprehensive definition and thus, confined the broader and wider application of term-socialism. He added, "I look upon it as a growing, dynamic conception, as something which is not rigid, as something which most fit in with the changing conditions of human life and activity in every country."[14]

Dimensions

It is clear by the fact that each country, which has experimented with it has modified socialism in the context of historical background, and made it conform to the actual state of the economic and political development and the social outlook of its people. According to Nehru, "Nothing is so foolish as to imagine that exactly the same processes take place in different countries with varying backgrounds."[15]

His thinking implies a clear distinction between the "universalistic content of socialism which would differ from country to country in accordance with the economic, social, cultural and political conditions of each country. He further stated, "I think Marx was a very great man and all of use can learn from Marx. But the point is that it is grossly unfair to ask Marx who belonged to the middle of 19th century to tell you what to do in the middle of the 20th century."[16]

Socialism is not a dogma which can be applied to any country irrespective of the conditions peculiar to it. Even the technique for attainment of socialism shall vary from country to country depending upon the objective conditions obtaining there in. He contributed to this idea and viewed that different countries at different stages of economic development shall have different techniques for the attainment of socialism.

According to Nehru even the form of socialism may differ radically from country to country depending upon their different stages of economic growth. Thus, socialism of the highly and industrially developed country shall vary from socialism of a less developed countries.

He further remarked, "It would be absurbed to talk of socialism to a villager who is not in a position to understand what it means."[18]

Socialism and Growth and Nehru

The various 'sums' that play such an important part in the world today - nationalism, liberalism, communism, imperalism, fascism, etc." are efforts on the part of various groups to answer these questions.[19]

Through years of thought Nehru evolved his own ideas about socialism and he developed a deep faith in the ultimate succes of socialism as the panacea of human ills of social and economic nature. He saw no way of ending the poverty, inequality, the chronic unemployment, problem of production and distribution of the people except through socialism. In ultimate analysis the value of socialism lay in its charming effect and healing power for all social and economic ills of the present day society.[20]

Nehru said, we have accepted socialism as our goal not only because it seems to us right and beneficial but because there is no other way for the solution of our economic problems.[21] If we want India to be prosperous, progress and standard of living to be raised, we must socialistic society in our country. He as such declared himself as:

"Well I stand for socialism and, I hope India will stand for socialism and that India will go towards the contribution of socialist state and I do believe that the whole world will have to go that way."[22] To Nehru, this should be the ideal of every sensible nation, society and individual. It should be the ideal of every sensible society or of individual. Nehru had been compelled to believe in it by the circumstances prevailing at the time of the great world crisis and slump. While other systems and theories have failed in analysing the causes. Marxism alone explained at more or less satisfactorily and offered real solutions.

Therefore, Nehru considered socialism as the inevitable step or panacea for the Socio-economic evils of the society prevailing in India.

Socialistic View of Nehru on Problem of Production and Distribution

The socialistic view of Jawaharlal Nehru on problem of production and distribution is still very useful. According to him, production means, extra wealth. If we do not produce we have not enough wealth[23] and the prosperity of a nation depends on its capacity for production.[24] But it became increasingly evident that production by itself does not solve our problems or lead to happiness and contenment. The passion for riches, for acquisition, for more and more wealth tends to corrupt and to create greater imbalances.[25]

The Industrial Revolution and capitalism solved the problem of production, but did not solve the problem of distribution, equitably, or the "new wealth created. So the old tussle between the haves and the have nots" remained the same rather it became acuter. Nehru remarked, "we must remember that poverty and want are no-longer economic necessities, although, under the present anarchic and capitalist system they may be inevitable. The world and our country produce enough or can produce enough for the masses to attain a high standard of well-being, but unhappily good things are concerned by a few and millian live in utter want.[26] It has made the difference between the luxury of the very rich and the poverty of the poor even greater than it was in the past.[27] The growth of inequality in the distribution of wealth, added to some other factors, led to the new struggle between labour and capital in the industrial countries.

In the opinion to Nehru, "the man who works should enjoy the fruits of his labour while the man who sits on the cushion should get nothing."[28] Consequently, the problem of equitable distribution on the right use of what is produced become important. It was not in the nature of capitalism to solve the problem of distribution. The problem of distribution was to be solved only through the process of elimination of entire capitalist structure of society.

Relevance

The more possible solution is a scientific system was offered by the socialism and it according to Nehru followed that there must not be big Zamindars and big factories must be owned by the state.[29]

This socialisation of means of production and distribution leads to the ending of private property, except in a restricted sense, the replacement of the present profit system by a higher level of co-operative service, a change in our instincts, habits and desires, the avoidance of private monopoly, a new civilization, radically different from the present capitalist order.[30]

Moreover, according to Nehru "private monopoly would be avoided and wages and salaries would be so adjusted as to give enough purchasing power to the community to consume all the goods produced. There can be no unemployment and there can be no trade slump."[31] In a socialist state trade becomes a state affair. A socialist state becomes self-producing and self-succient for which production is divided and allotted to different suitable areas. The produce is then exchanged for consumption. Nehru has observed that a socialist has a clear and scientific way-out of this maddle.

Problem of Inequality and Nehru

Like his other socialist brothren the conscience of Jawaharlal Nehru was being tortured by existing inequality and its corresponding evil effects on the human society. In this study of History, he understood the factors or forces which had to the origin and growth of inequality.

The wealth goes to those who are the managers or organisers, they usually get the lion's share of everything good.

According to Nehru, inequality arising from the exploitation of one class by another is a great social injustice which leads to the poverty of the exploited. The capitalism was based as perpetuating inequality and injustice.[32] The whole tendency of the capitalist system is to aggravate inequalities in the distribution of wealth.

This dynamic nature of tendency of inequalities caused by capitalism campelled Nehru to write, that today we see a society in which there are tremendous difference between man and of poor and man of rich and great poverty.

Some people live in luxury without doing anywork while others work from morning to night without no rest or leisure and yet have not got the barest necessaries of life.[33]

To him, there is also a greater disparity between these wealthy and powerful nations and the under-developed poor nations. This disparity has increased in recent years, inspite of the efforts to raise the level of under developed nations.[34] Consequent upon this, conflicts and dangers of war between these nations and social unrest have increased. Both result in fear and insecurity. These disparities whether between nations or within the nation, must be lessened.

Nehru clearly suggested that socialism is a panacea for the problem of inequality. He took a critical view of the economic inequality in modern society. To him, the whole of the 19th century civilization in Europe was based on the ideology of the French Revolution which was again based on the idea of the sacredness of private property. This ideology, with its slogan of political liberty equality and fraternity became completely out of date with the growth of industrial capitalism.

Political Liberty brought vote but it was gradually discovered that this was of little use when there was so much economic inequality. A starting man could do little with his vote and could be easily coerched and exploited.[35]

It is therefore, essential that economic equality should be aimed at for this control of means of production by the society and service restriction of private property and necessary. In short, all human being should have equal opportunity.

To Nehru, Liberty and democracy have no meaning without equality. Political freedom or political equality is the very basis on which you build up other equalities. At the same time, political equality may cease have meaning if there is gross economic inequality.[36]

Nehru was very conscious of the inequality between man and man, between group and group, between nation and nation, of biological inequality, and intellectual inequality.

Any attempt to equalise them in all respects will end in failure. Nehru rightly remarks, "one can't be too dogmatic about that too. You can't make every body equal for the simple reason that people are intellectually and physically different. These are clever, stupid and all types of people. But what you can do is to equalise opportunities for all and apply the same standard for everyone."[37]

To Nehru equality means equal opportunities for all and there should be no political economic or social barriers. He was of the view that not only equal opportunities must be given to all economic and cultural growth must be given to enforce backward individuals or groups or nations so as to enable then to catch up to those who are ahead of them.

Nehru suggested that if we face the problem we must root out the causes. So we should come back to the fundamental basis of socialism. We, moreoer, can't avoid socialism however, much we may dislike it. He further believed that if the diagnosis is correct then the disease must have a speedy and fatal end.

In other words, socialism means the nationalisation of the means of production and distribution so that whole state may be benefitted.

To sum up equality of opportunities, absence of exploitation of one by another, friendly co-operation with others are such ethical approaches to socialism which are the very foundation of Nehru utopian vision of society. The important thing is that every individual should be given equal opportunity in a more or less equalitarian society with no great inequalities or disparities at any rate now, so far as opportunity is concerned.[38]

According to him it is the crux of the problem in present day society. Socialism is the only solution of our present economic disparity and all our ills.

Problem of Exploitation and Nehru

Inequality, arising from the exploitation of one individual by another or one class by another or even one country by another country, is a great social injustice because it leads to the poverty. According to Nehru the capitalist system of social structure is based on exploitation. Methods of exploitation may differ from age to age, but the spirit is the same.[39]

He was of the opinion that system was more responsible than individual for exploitation. He cleared with various examples that exploitation is not the fault of the persons exploiting.

The socialist theory was that the state, representing society as a whole, should own and control the means of production. Socialists were, according to Nehru, agreed that anything which could be used for making private profit out of other people's work should be socialized that is made the property of the state.[40]

If the people as a whole choose to exploit themselves they perfectly welcome to do so, but even so the benefits go to them as a whole and not to selected groups or individuals. According to Nehru, there will be no surplus in a properly ordered and planned society and whatever is produced not for profit, but will go towards raising the standard of living of the people as a whole. He further expressed that the workers have to share in the prosperity of the nation not only they should get the fruits of his toil. Otherwise, there will be continuous dissatisfacion and tension.

As such, "on exploitation of workers by the capitalists must be stopped, the man who works should enjoy the fruits of his labour while the man who sits on the cushion should get nothing. In socialism according to Nehru no one should be ideal and that the man who works harder should get more, while the man who works less should get less, that is, payment according to the work done. This was the ideal plan. Thus, he repeatedly stated that the Socialism is the only solution of many ills.

Problem of Poverty and Nehru

Nehru was very much critical over poverty prevailing in our society. According to his views poverty was the worst enemy of mankind because it constitutes danger to prosperity everywhere. In otherwords, it is not only danger to prosperity it is rather danger to national and international peace.

Consequently, it is the prime objective of the socialism to remove poverty. The whole tendency of the capitalist system is to aggravate inequalities by exploiting other and thereby making poverty in the society, but to Nehru, the economics of scarcity has no meaning in the world of the day. Our economic policy must therefore, first aim at plenty and then at equality.[41]

He was of the view that wealth need not mean gold and silver but wealth in goods and services. The capitalist could only think of scarcity. Our economic policy must therefore, aim at plenty.

There is prevailing notion that there are rich and poor. The rich and poor have existed all along from the very begining of history so capitalist should not be blamed for the present crisis. He said, "We must remember that poverty and wants are no longer economic necessities, although under the present anachic capitalist system they may be inevitable."[42]

He further stated that "Personally I dislike the praise of poverty and suffering. I do not think they are at all desirable, and they ought to be abolished.

Gandhiji laid stress on the rich treating these riches as a trust for people. For Nehru, it was a view point of considerable anitquity and one comes across it frequently is India as well as medieval Europe. According to Nehru, "I confess that I have always been wholly unable to understand how many persons can reasonably expect this it happen, or imagine that there in lies the solution of the social problem."[43]

It would be unfair to give unchecked power and wealth to an individual and expect him to use it entirely for the public good. The snobbery of birth position and economic power in perpetuated and the consequences in many ways are disastrous.[44]

The sole trusteeship that can be fair is the trusteeship of the nation and not of one individual or group. Nehru was convinced that the state representing society as a whole should assume the responsibility of the economy as a whole also. According to him, the socialist theory was that the state representing the society as a whole, should own and control the means of production that is, land and factories etc. The problem of poverty can't be solved except by socialism.

Historically, he was convinced that socialism is bound to come and according to him it is the only panacea for the poverty and other economic and social ills. He has not seen any way of ending the poverty, the vast unemployment the degradation and the subjection of the Indian people except through socialist.[45]

Problem of Unemployment and Nehru

Problem of unemployment is a terrific human problem which we can't ignore, if we ignore it then peril is inevitable. Unemployment always retards the progress of a country. This problem is of immense importance. According to Nehru, the prosperity of a nation is judged by the number of people who are unemployed. Unemployment is the bane of a nation.

In the opinion of Nehru, it was wrong to think that the government services are there to maintain the people. In advanced countries, it is no honour to be a government servant, it is only in backward countries where there is a great deal of unemployment, that government services are given undue importance.

In his opinion, the present socio-economic structure of the world has completely failed to solve this problem. It has no solution for it. So, it is the inevitable result of the failure of capitalism.[46]

This restriction of mass purchasing power by keeping down the wages and salaries under the capitalistic structure of society, creates a "Vicious Circles" leading to unemployment on mass scale. The low mass purchasing power means low consumption level i.e. low demand in the market for consumption goods which compells to reduce production and it leads retrenchment or lessening of working hours which finally results in mass scale unemployment which means again low purchasing power and the circle will comlete.

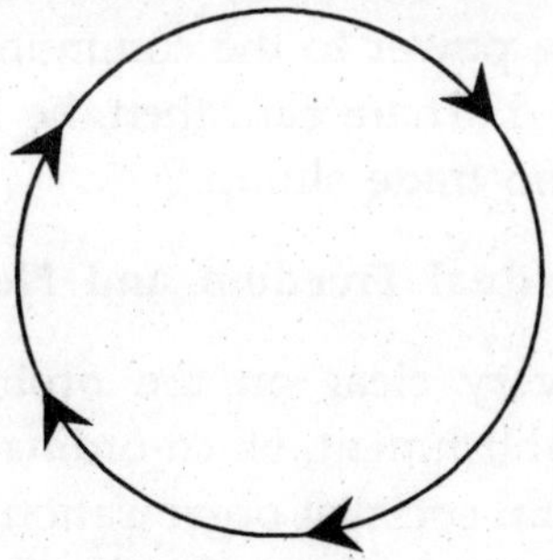

According to him capitalists add vastly to the wealth of the world but this wealth is largely concentrated in a few nations and a few hands on the other hand, there is a continuous improvement in technique, the method of production leading to greater mechanisation, for greater production and more unemployment as workers were replaced by machinery. And this led to curious result.[47]

He rightly further observed that the present capitalistic economic structure of the world has failed completely in solving this problem of unemployment. To him, in order to solve that problem of unemployment,whether of the middle class or of the peasantry or of the industrial workers, you have to go outside that frame and picture, and think in different terms and lay down different boundaries.[48]

We can't produce employment by legislation. But our economic approach must be such that we can reach the stage of full employment within a measurable period of time. Our steps must be aimed at that. To do so fully would to adopt socialism, but capitalists are not likely to do that till circumstances compel them socialism is the only alternative offered to us which is state ownership of the means of production and distribution. We can't escape the choice and if we really care for a better order of society and for ending the exploitation of man by man, we can not but cast our weight on the side of socialism. Private monopoly would be avoided and wages and salaries would be so adjusted as to give enough purchasing power to the community to consume all the goods produced. There can, then, be no unemployment and there can be no trade slump.[49]

Problem of Individual Freedom and Nehru

Nehru was very clear on the problem of individual freedom. The establishment of co-ordination between two conception of central socialist organisation of society and the state with the greatest amount of individual freedom. In his opinion socialism was the best remedy for maintaining the balance between the two Nehru believed that socialism could be democratic and not authoritarian. In his words,

"I do not see why under socialism there should not be a great deal of freedom for the individual.... Above all he will have the freedom which comes from economic security."[50] He further added, "I hope that socialism does not kill individually." It will release innumerable individuals from economic and cultural bondage.[51] In socialism every body should have an opportunity to rise which is possible only in socialism according to him.

After all, all individual freedom is not an end in itself. The individual must not infringe on the freedom of other individuals. It is perfectly true that there can be no perfect freedom for an individual or nation.

Problem of Unjust and Evils of Social Customs and Nehru

A Nehru was in favour of discarding and eradication of social evils like economic bondage, untouchability unjust customs and habits which are human parasites.

A. Nehru on Economics Bondage

According to him social reform legislations is good and to be worked for and welcomed. He accepted the fact that in all our attempts at social reforms the economic factor is forgotten. He suggested to eradicate the evil like economic bondage.[52]

B. Nehru on Human Parasites

According to Nehru Joint Hindu family system was the root cause of human paracites which must go like many customs and tradition. He said, "ultimate solution lies in a complete refashioning of our society. He accepted that the number of paracites was very large i.e. Zamindars, Sadhu-Fakirs" etc. They do not work or contribute and are burden to the society.

C. Nehru on Untouchability

He expressed his view that untouchability, prevailing in the society must be stopped. The problem of untouchability and harizans could be approached in different way. For socialist it present no difficulty. There can be no differentiation or victimisation Economically speaking, the Harizans have constituted the landless proletrate and an economic solution removes the social barriers that customs and tradition have raised.[53]

He further added that we shall continue our fight against the course of untouchability and other forms of enforced inequality and shall especially try to help those who are economically otherwise backward.[54] He proclaimed, "Broadly speaking I imagine that such problems could be easier dealt with in a socialist structure of society."[55] He was of an idea that the solution to these social evils lies through socialism, whether one likes or dislikes, if these problems are not solved, the world will be threatened with chaos.[56]

To him, "Socialism may good or bad, it may be dream of the distant future, or a problem of the present; whatever it is or might be, it seems to occupy a large corner of the mind of the world today."[57] He stated that today welfare state and even a classless society are not ideals of socialism, but are accepted by capitalist countries also, even though the approaches are different, he realised that socialism was the only panacea of economic, social and political ills prevailing in the present day society.

'Socialistic Pattern of Society' and Nehru

Mahatma Gandhi, Sardar Vallabh Bhai Patel and Pt. Jawaharlal Nehru stressed India to freedom but differed widely enough in there views on to the way the economy of Independent India could best he organised. Gandhiji was profoundly distrustful of the large units of a machine based urban economy and believed that industry should be directly linked to the 7,00,000 village of country for eradication of poverty and unemployment. Sardar Patel saw nothing wrong in mass production by factory methods and all the other attributes of modern capitalism. Pandit Jawaharalal Nehru was for socialism but the knew that little could be done in this direction until political freedom was attained, so Nehru moved more rapidly in this context.

As earlier mentioned Nehru had a pragmatic and non-doctrinaire approach to Socialistic pattern of society. Economic and social policy has to be shaped from time to time in the light of historical circumstances. It was neither necessary nor desirable that the economy should become a monolithic type or organisation offering little play for experiment. He himself stated, While delivering himself before the third meeting of the National Development Council on November 9, 1954 he stated as follows:

"The picture I have to mind is definitely and absolutely a socialistic pattern of society. I am not using the word in a dogmate sense at all, but in the sense of meaning largely that the means of production should be socially owned and controlled for the benefit of society as a whole."[58]

We have deliberately laid down as our subjective a 'Socialistic pattern of Society', though we have not precisely defined it.

Nehru did not approach this problem in any rigid or doctrinaire way. There is no lack of firmness and rigidity about the ideals aimed at because there must be some fixity, if we want India to progress, if we want India to be prosperous and if we want to raise the standards of India, we want a socialist society in India. There is no lack of firmness about that.

Nehru had no difficulty in making the two Houses of Parliament to adopt the "Socialistic Pattern of Society" as the goal of Indian democracy. In the Annual Session of Congress Party at Avadi (January, 1995) he made it clear that "Planning should take place with a view to the establishment of a socialistic pattern of society".

The inauguration of the Second Plan in 1956 he related a new era in which creation of a capital goods or producer goods industry rather than the development of prosperous agriculture as the base of our economy, became the aim of Indian Planning.

Therefore, the concept of socialistic pattern of society is not conceived in a doctrinaire sense. The slogans of yesterday have little meaning in the present context whether the slogans are capitalistic, socialistic or communistic.[59] The system evolved by Nehru was consciously directed towards the welfare of the common man rather than towards enrichment of the few.

According to Nehru, it aims at the establishment of a society whose pattern in only socialistic, nor of a society which is basically socialist, as ordained by orthodox socialist thinkers. To Nehru, socialistic pattern of society is a phrase which means in one word, socialistic. But in Nehru's view, they all are exactly the something without the slightest difference.[60]

Further, he was firm in his belief that we can bring about social changes and developments by the pressure of democracy and also by a friendly co-operative approach, rather than the approach of struggle and elimination.

The key word pattern, is deed, in the governing factor in determining the quantum of socialism to be grafted on Indian economy. A society of this kind does not exist in the world to guide as a precedent such a fluid state of affairs tends to create discord in social thought which in turn retards the growth of emotional integration without which dynamism of spirit in pursuit of any programme for national reconstruction can hardly be possible. He himself observed that too much vagueness also comes in the way of effective action.

The Indian National Congress had always thought in terms of some socialistic pattern. The principles involved were work for increasing production for raising the standard of living and having progressively fuller employment so as to achieve full employment. The machinery of the state was directed towards implementing the above objectives. In this policy shaft, Pt. Nehru was guided by a fellow traveller, Prof. P.C. Mahalanobis who was appointed Statistical Advisor to the Planning Commission.

He further defined 'socialistic pattern of society'.

"We believe in democracy and inequality and in the removal of special privileges and we have set ourselves the goal of developing a socialistic pattern of society in our country through peaceful methods. Whatever shape that pattern of democracy might take it must lead to open access to knowledge and equal opportunity to all."[61]

In other words production of more extra wealth was the primary function of growing society. He thus stated that "In order to reach equality, as I hope we shall some times or other we need not follow the road of some artificial fixation of ceilings but a hundred paths which gradually take us there.[62] He himself remarked, "In order to reach equality I hope we shall sometimes or other, we need not follow the road of some artificial fixation of ceilings but a hundred paths which gradually take us there. An artificial attempt may indeed, prevent us from reaching it."[63]

Pt. Nehru further stressed that the Second Five Year Plan must keep the national aims of a welfare state and socialistic economy before it, which can be achieved by the considerable increase in national income. Consequently, our national economic policy must, therefore, aim at plenty and equitable distribution. He warned the indian planners that these objectives should be based on the physical needs of the people.

Difference Between Welfare State & Socialistic Pattern of Society

He tried to differentiale the two words convening the same meaning, 'the welfare state' and 'socialistic pattern of society'. According to Nehru both the cooncepts are not synonymous. It is true that a socialistic economy must provide for a welfare state but it does not necessarily follow that a welfare state must also be based on a socialistic pattern of society.

It is obvious, according to him that the establishment of a welfare state is not enough, welfare state may increase the national wealth, but it does not necessarily lead to equal-distribution of opportunities and equitable distribution.

The welfare state and the socialistic economy were to be fused together. In such a society, the principal means of production under social ownership or control, production is progressively speed up and there is equitable distribution of the national wealth.[64]

Aims and Objectives of Socialistic Pattern of Society

There is novelty regarding aims and objectives of socialistic pattern of society. It still continued to be a classless and casteless society providing greater facilities to individuals better opportunities for their uplift and getting them out of the acquisitive society, as he observed that we have accepted in India as our objective a socialistic pattern of society. It means not only economic organisation but something deeper which involves a way of Thinking and living. The acquisitive society, whose chief aim is profit making, not only brings conflict in its train but it opposed to the basic urge of modern man for social justice.[65]

He, in this context, stated that "we have deliberately laid down as our objective a socialist pattern of society. Personally I think that the acquisitive society, which is the base of capitalism, is no longer suited to the present age. We have to evolve a high order more in keeping with modern trends and foundations and involving not so much competition but much greater co-operation.[66]

The economic pattern of Jawaharlal Nehru which is described as the socialistic pattern of society represents an attempt to create a mixed economy which combines private enterprise with government planning, overall direction and control, as well as government initiative in fields that private entrepreneurs might not find attractive. He has envisaged for India a new type of economic life distinct in itself and identified neither with the "Laissez faire" economics of the 19th century no the patterned totalitarianism of Soviet Russia or China or Nazi Germany. In his words, "I would beg of you not to imagine that because socialism conceives of nationalized industry, therefore, you must have all industry nationalised. I think that as the socialistic pattern grows, there is bound to be more and more nationalised industry, but what is important is not that there should be an attempt to nationalize everything, but that we should aim at the ultimate result, which is higher production and employment. If by taking any step you actually hinder the process of production and employment from growing, then that does not lead you to the socialistic pattern."[67]

According to him no body believes in Laissez-faire. There was regulation and control all over the world in regard to the industry and foreign trade (i.e. imports & exports). Everywhere, even in the most highly developed economics of the capitalist economy, the state functions in a way which possibly a socialist fifty years ago did not dream of.

As such, his emphasis was not on state capitalist or collectivism, and concentration of economic activity in the hands of the state, but freedom of initiative and enterprise wherever necessary. He further explained that the economic system that he had in view was one of a democratic collectivism. As far as possible there should be freedom to choose one's occupation.[68]

However, while addressing the National Development

Council he emphasised on less of concentration through leaving sufficient room for private enterprise and categorically laying stress on the democratic and peaceful means. He said "I do not see any harm at all, in fact, I see a lot of good in the private functioning."[69]

Thus, his emphasis was on democratic method, individual freedom and dignity of the individual. He was of the opinion that "I think, this method is in the long him much more successful even from the point of view of time and more so from the point of view of final results."[70] According to him all individuals in India must have equal opportunities of growth from birth onwards, and equal opportunities for work according to their capacity, the dimensions of the socialistic objective began to grow greate in his thought.

Nehru had deeper interest in defining India's socialist objectives and socialistic pattern of society instead of socialism pure and simple as appeared from his views expressed during sessions of All India Congress Committee in 1963 at Jaipur and in 1964 at Bhubaneshwar. In these session, the objective of the Congress was defined as "democratic socialism". It was generally agreed at that time that Jawaharlal Nehru was the moving central force behind the resolution even to the Avadi resolution was far mixed.

REFERENCES

1. *Selected Works of Jawaharlal Nehru*, Vol. III, 1972, p. 250.

2. *Ibid.*, Vol. VII, 1975, p. 181.

3. Rao, V.K.R.V., *The Nehru Legacy*, Popular Prakashan, Bombay, 1971, p. 69.

4. Shah, A.B., *Jawaharlal Nehru: A Critical Tribale*, Manantalla, Bombay, 1965, p. 20.

5. *Nehru Jawaharlal Eighteen Months of India*, 1938, pp. 29-30.

6. Karanjia, R.K., *The Philosophy of Mr. Nehru*, Allen & Unwin, London, 419.

7. Nehru Jawaharlal, *Glimpses of World History*, 1949, p. 543.

8. *Selected Works of Jawaharlal Nehru, op. cit.*, Vol. VII, p. 271.

9. *Ibid.*, Vol. VI, 1974, pp. 124-25.

10. Nehru Jawaharlal, *(EMI) Eighteen Months of India, op. cit.*, p. 14.

11. Nehru Jawaharlal, *Glimpses of World History, op. cit.*, p. 540.

12. Nehru Jawaharlal, *Speeches of Jawaharlal Nehru, op. cit.*, Vol. III, 1970, p. 52.

13. Sen N.B. (Ed.), *Wit and Wisdom of Jawaharalal Nehru*, 1960, p. 156.

14. Krishnamurti, Y.G., *Jawaharlal Nehru—The Man and His Ideas*, Popular Book Depot, Bombay, 1944.

15. Nehru Jawaharlal, *The Unity of India*, 1948, p. 18.

16. Nehru Jawaharlal, *Speeches, op. cit.*, Vol. III, 1970, p. 84.

    And Glimpses of World History, 1949, p. 932.

    An Autobiography, 1962, p. 128.

17. Nehru Jawaharlal, *Speeches*, Vol. III, 1970, p. 52.

18. *Selected Works of Jawaharlal Nehru*, Vol. VII, 1975, *op. cit.*, p. 226.

19. Nehru Jawaharlal, *Glimpses of World History, op. cit.*, 1949, p. 801.

20. Bright J.S. (CED), *Speeches of Jawaharlal Nehru*, Vol. I, 1945, p. 102.

21. Nehru Jawaharlal, *Speeches, op. cit.*, Vol. IV, 1964, p. 5.

22. Kausik, P.D., *Congress Ideology and Programme*, Allied Publication, Bombay, 1964, p. 349.

23. Mukherjee, Hiren, *Nehru on Socialism*, Manisa Gram Thalya, Calcutta, 1964, pp. 66-68.

24. Brecher, Michael, *Nehru: A Political Biography*, Oxford University Press, London, 1969, pp. 591-92.

25. *Ibid.*, India and The World, 1962, p. 34.

26. *Selected Works of Jawaharlal Nehru*, Vol. III, 1972, p. 222.

27. *Nehru Jawaharlal, Glimpses of World History, op. cit.*, p. 346.

28. *Selected Works of Jawaharlal Nehru, op. cit.*, 1973, Vol. IV, p. 250.

29. *Ibid.*, Vol. III, 1972, p. 252.

30. Chibber, *Jawaharlal Nehru*, Vikas Publications, Delhi, 1970, p. 149.

31. Nehru Jawaharlal, *Eighteen Months of India, op. cit.*, 1938, pp. 193-94.

32. *Selected Works, op. cit.*, Vol. VI, p. 22, 1974.

33. *Ibid.*, p. 218, Vol. III, 1972.

34. Rao, V.K.R.V., Planning without Dogma in a Study of Nehru by Rafique Zakaria, A *Times of India* Publication, Bombay, 1960, pp. 304-14.

35. *Selected Works on J.N.*, Vol. III, 1972, p. 180.

36. Torman Cousins, Talks, 1951 and Jawaharlal Nehru, *The Unity of India*, 1948, p. 117.

37. Karanjia, R.K., *Interview with Jawaharlal Nehru*, 1960, p. 38.

38. Karanjia, R.K., *The Philosophy of Mr. Nehru*, Allen & Univ. London, 1962, p. 71.

39. Nehru Jawaharlal, *Glimpses of World History*, 1949, p. 337.

40. Sarin, L.N., *Jawaharlal Nehru*, S. Chand & Co. Delhi, 1968, p. 7.

41. *Speeches of Jawaharlal Nehru, op. cit.*, 1970, pp. 17-18.

42. *Selected Works on Jawaharlal Nehru, op. cit.*, Vol. III, 1972, p. 222.

43. Nehru Jawaharlal, *An Autobiography, op. cit.*, 1962, p. 192.

44. Brigh, J.S. (Ed.), *Before and After Independence*, speeches delivered by Jawaharlal Nehru, 1922-50, p. 399.

45. *Selected Works on Jawaharlal Nehru, op. cit.*, Vol. VII, 1975, p. 181.

46. Mahelanobis P.C., In National Herald, A New Approach in a Study of Nehru by Rafique Zakaria, A *Times of India* Publication, Bombay, 1964, p. 314.

47. Loksabha Secretariat, Jawaharlal Nehru's Speech in Parliament, 1953, p. 107.

48. Rao, Amitya, *Jawaharlal Nehru: Prime Minister*, Sterling Press, New Delhi, 1974, p. III.

49. Mehta Ashok, *Social Justice and National Development*, Popular Prakashan, Bombay, 1969, p. 121.

50. Nehru Jawaharlal, *The Unity of India, op. cit.*, 1948, p. 118.

51. Nehru Jawaharlal, *A Bunch of Old Letters*, 1960, p. 368.

52. *Selected Works on Jawaharlal Nehru, op. cit.*, Vol. II, 1975, p. 182.

53. *Speeches of Jawaharlal Nehru, op. cit.*, Vol. I, 1967, p. 4.

54. Nehru Jawaharlal, *The Unity of India, op. cit.*, 1948, p. 22.

55. Karanjia, R.K., *op. cit.*, 196, pp. 35-36.

56. *Selected Works or Jawaharlal Nehru*, Vol. VII, 1975, p. 246.

57. Nehru Jawaharlal, *Eighteen Months of India, op. cit.*, 1933, p. 229.

58. *Speeches of Jawaharlal Nehru, op. cit.*, 1964, p. 134.

59. Nehru Jawaharlal, *Planning & Development*, 1956, p. 28.

60. *Speeches of Jawaharlal Nehru, op. cit.*, 1970, Vol. III, p. 85.

61. *Ibid.*, pp. 302-303.

62. Nehru Jawaharlal, *A Study in Ideology and Social Change*, R.P. Dube, *op. cit.*, p. 216.

63. Publication Division, *Jawaharlal Nehru's Speeches*, 1949-53, Vol. II, Govt. of India, p. 306.

64. *The Hindu*, January 20, 1955, p. 5.

65. *Speeches of Jawaharlal Nehru, op. cit.*, Vol. IV, 1964, p. 170.

66. Kissin, Abdul Karim, A Maker of History: An Essay in A Study of Nehru by Rafique Zakaria, A *Times of India* Publication 1960, p. 91.

67. *Ibid.*, Vol. III, p. 12.

68. Nehru Jawaharlal, *Discovery of India*, 1972, p. 522.

69. *Speeches of Jawaharlal Nehru*, Vol. II, 1970, p. 13, *op. cit.*, 1956, p. 17.

4

Nehru on Public Sector

Introduction

Jawaharlal Nehru was the great advocate of Public Sector in Indian context. He was of the view that without growth of public sector it was vertually impossible to increase the economic growth of a poor economy like India. It was only due to the fact that he was aware that though, our economic potential was great, its conversion into finished wealth would need much mechanical and technological change and according to him industrialisation involves those basic changes that accompany the mechanization of an enterprise the big machine is but a tool to be used for good or ill.[1] On the other occasion he said, industrialism means the use of machinery of tools to lessen human labour and it seems a little reasonable to blame our tools when the fault lies with us in missing term. Nehru as such, defined "industrialisation means money and the control of the banking system in the country."[2] Several factors are conducive to industrialization. However, their applicability and effectiveness differ from one under-developed country to another depending among other things upon its industrial status, its size and resources, the relative incidence of the obstacle and the extent to which its government is prepared to guide or participate in its economic life. The difference in the process of industrial development between our country and the other may be due to variation in range, quality and availability of local natural resources. Lack of natural resources is likely to be an effective barrier to intensive and extensive industrialisation. According to Nehru, in India also we have, by and large many of the raw materials required.[3]

The developing countries suffer most from the shortage of capital. In general, industrialisation requires substantially more capital than an agricultural or commercial unit. The shortage of capital is due to the fact that in most of the underdeveloped countries the mass of population have little or no margin between income and expenditure that only a small number is regularly in receipt of income which permits saving.[4]

He was aware that though, our economic potential was great, its conversion into finished wealth would need much mechanical and technological aid. We should, therefore, gladly welcome such aid and co-operation on terms that were of mutual benefit. We believe that this may well help in the solution of the larger problems that confront the world. But we did not seek any material advantage in the exchange for any part of our hard own freedom he indeed, did not see why we should be afraid of accepting the kind of aid that helps us to progress more rapidly. He was prepared to take it but not for indefinite time, he stated that self-help was the first condition of success for a nation, no less than for an individual. He further added, "I think it is impossible for us to progress without having those basic things."[5]

Nehru wanted real freedom. In his opinion real freedom is not merely political freedom, rather it is economic freedom for the vast masses of our country, their having higher standard of living and putting an end to gross difference in wealth and opportunities. To him, an industrial base means basic industries, mother industries, heavy industries and the like. As soon as that established smaller industries flow from them and the rates of progress becomes fast. He was of that view the planning commission of India seeks to lay the foundations of an industrial structure by building the basic and heavy industries also all by producing electric power, middle and small scale industries will inevitably come in their train. His view point was that industrialisation produces machines, steel, power etc. which are the base. He advocated three fundamental requirements for industrialisation.

— heavy engineering and machine-making industries.

— scientific research institutes and

— development of electric power

In his opinion, it was always a difficult matter to balance the needs of today and the needs of tomorrow or the day after. But the government has to do it and industry also ought to do it. They have to think ahead.

On Industrialisation

Jawaharlal Nehru strongly stressed this solid foundation upon which the edifice of industrialisation can be built. In his view, the work of laying this solid foundation does not generally attract private industrialists because it does not pay for years to come. They would like a return on Capital within a year or two. Thus, in a country like ours the burden of development falls on government. He of course, welcomed private capital and private enterprise but the responsibility for development, as he stated, falls on government. The conditions are quite different in developed countries like America. But in India it has become inevitable, if we have to build on solid foundations and go up, government must be a party to it. The public sector thus becomes very important.[7]

While giving strong emphasis on heavy and machine making industries, Nehru also welcomed the role played by small scale cottage industries in the development of the national economy is they provide larger scale employment, ensure a more equitable distribution of national income, and facilitate an effective mobilization to the resources of capital and skill which might otherwise remain unutilised. As such, to him small scale industries must also be developed simultaneously in broad scheme of industrialisation.[8] He firmly advocated that India must be industrialised as rapidly as possible. An industrialisation consists of all kinds of industries - major, middle, small, village and cottage.[9] Moreover, in his mind, there was no essential conflict between the two.[10]

Role of Public Sector and Nehru

He was of the opinion that modern warfare is becoming more and more mechanised, it is well known fact that no nation which has not got a sufficiently developed industrial back ground, can hope to carry on a war effectively for any length of time. He realised that even from defence point of view, industrialisation, particularly through public sector is must. He was of opinion that the process of industrialisation can be acceperated by utilising the modern scientific technology of production. He had deep faith in Science and technology. He strongly supported development of science, the growth of basic mother industry and the use of up-to-date, modern advanced, and higher productive technology. He stated, "Not for the sake of merely having a big factory or a big machine, but for human betterment of the people of India."[11] He was well convinced that we can't progress without industrialisation with higher techniques. We can not produce enough without modernising or methods of production.

According to Jawaharlal Nehru public sector occupies a key role in our economic activities, it is an essential and vital part of our economy. It is an engine for growth for social justice and instrument for regional development for laying the foundation of strong India. He further made it clear that it was expected to be the principal agent for rapid economic and social transformation by developing infra-structure and the core sector. He conceived public sector as the kingpin of all our developmental efforts, not only in the strict sense of economic growth but more so in the type of society and social relations that were envisaged for the nation. Rapid transformation of the Indian economy on modern lines, ensuring social justice and avoiding sharp inequalities together with rising, levels of consumption, this sums up the goal of our planned national endeavour. The public sector has to play a vital role in realising each one of these goals. The role of public sector enterprises can't therefore be marginal or peripheral. It has to be decisive and crucial.[12]

Objectives of Public Sector

According to Nehru the main objectives of public sector were:

(a) helping in the rapid economic growth and industrialisation of the country and creating necessary infrastructure for economic development.

(b) earning returns on investments and generating resources for development;

(c) promoting redistribution of income and wealth;

(d) creating employment opportunities;

(e) promoting balanced regional development;

(f) assisting the development of small scale and ancillary industries; and

(g) remoting import substitution, saving and earning foreign exchange for the economy.[13]

Nehru's Arguments

Nehru advocated public sector's need in Indian context in the following terms:

(i) creation of infra-structure for balanced economic growth,

(ii) rapid economic development of Indian economy;

(iii) check on concentration of wealth and economic power;

(iv) arrangement of adequate finances for development programmes and national building activities;

(v) creation of enormous employment opportunities;

(vi) acquisitian of sick units and their better management;

(vii) social control on long-term capital with the help of public financial institutions;

(viii) balanced regional develoopment and corrective regional imbalances;

(ix) proper development and expansion of private sector; and

(x) import substitution and export promotion.

Indian Context

Consequent upon these factors, Nehru advocated public sector for Indian economy as to:

(a) achieve economic justice by controlling the principal means of production;

(b) ensure the well being of all citizens;

(c) present the exploitation of one person by another or of one group by another; and

(d) to present the accumulation of wealth to an extent which inconsistent with the existence of classics society.[14]

Role of State

The state sector plays not only a decisive role but is also pre-requisite of a successful materialisation of the economic policies. It has twin objectives.

(i) providing all opportunities to the private sector and

(ii) developing industries of base strategic importance.

However, state sector considered as its main responsibility to assist, encourage and to give all its support to the private sector of all categories, big medium and small and monopoly capital trying its utmost to get major share.

Soon after independence, there was a widespread belief that without increasing the role of the state, it was not possible either to accelerate the process of growth or to create an industrial base for substained economic development of the country. The Second Five Year plan stated in unequivoçal terms.

"The adoption of the socialist pattern of society an the national objective, as well as the need for planned and rapid develoopment, require that all industries of basic and strategic importance, or in the nature of a public utility services, should be in the public sector. The state has, therefore, to assure direct responsibility for the future development of industries over a wide area."

Strategy of Nehru

The Second Plan further emphasised: The public sector has to expand rapidly. It has not only to initiate developments which the private sector is either unwilling thing or unable to undertake, it has to play the dominant role in shaping the entire pattern of investment in the economy, whether it makes the investment directly or whether these are mode by the private sector. The private sector has to play its part within the framework of the comprehensive plan accepted by the community.[16]

Outlining the strategy of development, the Second Plan further opined, "The use of modern technology requires large scale production and a unified control and allocation of resources in certain major lines of activity. These include exploitation of minerals and basic and capital goods industries which are major determinants of the rate of growth of the economy. The responsibility for new developments in these fields must be undertaken in the main by the state and the existing units have to fall in line with the emerging pattern....... In a growing economy which gets increasingly diversified there is scope for both public and private sectors to expand simultaneously, but it is inevitable, if development is proceed at the peace envisaged and to contribute effectively to the attainment of the larger scale ends in view, that the public sector must grow not only absolutely but also relatively to the private sector."[17]

Certain Issues

Accorrding to Nehru from the above citations, certain issues stand out clearly.

(i) The consensus on the eve of second plan was that all industries of basic and strategic importance should be in the public sector.

(ii) The public sector was to act as a senior partner in the process of development and undertake investments in such areas in which private sector was unwilling or unable to undertake such investments.

(iii) In the exploration of minerals and basic & capital goods industries and infrastructure public sector has to undertake direct responsibility.

(iv) while accepting the framework of the mixed economy, public sector was expected to contribute effectively to the social ends in view and grow at a fast rate so that the share of public sector grows both absolutely and relatively to the private sector.

This was a welcome decision because at that time, the Indian private sector did not either possess the capability or the resources to undertake tumpy investments in the capital goods sector. Private sector was also not willing to undertake responsibility of the infrastructure. Thus, to initiate the process of building an industrial base and to reduce our dependence industrial nations, it was considered desirable that the State should develop the capital goods sector which was a totally rejected area during the British period.

According to Nehru "A state is supposed to perform that every state is trying to do very much more for the individual than has ever been attempted before. So the State becomes more and more of a socially functioning organism for the good of society or the individual, as you like.[18]

If the state and individual are properly integrated and organised there is no conflict otherwise, if one side goes ahead of the other there is a lack of balance.[19]

In illustrating his concept of the socially functioning organism, Nehru goes on to advocate that "the state, apart from protecting the individual from foreign enemies or internal disorder, has the duty to undertake to provide him with opportunities of progress of education, health, sanitation—generally, everything that would give him the opportunity of following himself for such work as he is capable of. This obsiously leads the modern state to grow more and more centralized. But such a tendency appears to Nehru as a deep problem of the time. One can not escape centralized authority, whether it is of state, of the big corporation, of the trade union, or of any group. The difficulty which confronts Nehru is: all centralization is a slight encroachment on the freedom of the individual or but at the same time understands the impossibility of escaping centralization in modern society. Nehru attempts to find an answer to the problem of the conflict between centralization and individual freedom. State cannot do without a large measure of centralization.

Basic Functions of State

In this light, Nehru thinks of the basic functions of the state.[20]

(i) State has to try and function in such a way as to provide for the primary needs of the people as at any rate, to make such arrangements that people can obtain those primary needs.

(ii) These are the important secondary needs. As regards economic organisation, Nehru believes in a flexible policy, especially with regard to his own country.

Where private resources are not abundant, he says, any project should be a state project. Sinc schemes like river valley projects or similar large works can't be undertakes by individuals, they must be state schemes if they are to be done at all. Certain other large projects can either be state projects or jointly owned by the state and private enterprise, with a measure of state control, but leaving a large field for private enterprise.

Private and Public Sectors

He says, "What I would call a public sector of our economy and a private sector and may be a sector where the two overlap, with part state control and largely private sector managing. Under state control so, we have these three branches of our economy, there need not be any rigid lines between them and we can see which functions better and more successfully and allow them to develop."[21]

Nehru feels that as a state increases its centralization in certain sections of the national economy, it becomes all the more important to safeguard and increase the right of the individuals. So far as the political rights of the individual are concerned, he wants them to be safeguarded by the constitution of the state. So far as economic questions are concerned, it is a question of a state interfering to protect rather than keeping away, because in rather under-developed economies there is a tendency in certain groups of vested interests to over-ride the interests of the large groups by whatever methods they have."[22]

Nehru keeps it uppermost in his mind that the state exists to serveman. Political liberty, which a modern democratic state in proud to give to its people, is not an end in itself but is the means by which economic and social freedom may be attained. It is a function of the state to help develop all aspects of human happiness. To Nehru, development of man is the ultimate aim of the state.

In person one begins to appreciate the Marxian theory, that the state is really the coercive apparatus meant to enforce the will of a group that controls the government.[23]

Nehru believes it as fundamentally true that civilization has been build up on co-operation and for bearance and mutual collaboration in a fine way. Thus, the force, the compulsion and the violenc of the governing group constitute more or less the basic nature of the state.[24]

His Scientific Approach

To Nehru, in his scientific approach to the questions of force and violence, some kind of state coercion appears inevitable. In one sense or another all life, according to Nehru, is full of conflict and violence. "Violence is the very life blood of the modern state and social system. The national state itself exists because of offensive and defensive violence."[25]

As regards good government, a good government according to Nehru, can be judged by greater efficiency in production, consumption and the activities which goes to raise the physical, the spiritual and the standards of the masses. His faith in good government was absolute "I believe that self government is good for any country, but I am not prepared to accept even self government at the cost of real good government."[26]

Basic Policies

Thus, whatever the basic policy pursued by a country, it becomes inevitable for the governmental structure to become involved in social problems ever increasingly.[27] The burden of modern government being so increasingly heavy. Nehru ultimately looks for the co-operation of the people for the success of government. To him, freedom brings its own responsibilities and burdens and they can only be shouldered in the spirit of a free people, self disciplined and determined to preserve and enlarge that freedom.[28]

More activities of the government must be right and should not and end only within the arbit of governmental principles, because "It is the activity of the people, it is the temper of the people and the co-operation that the people in general give that will solve these problems this way or that. He believed that ultimately all problems concerning human beings and their mutual relations depend on the character of human beings. He advocated complete co-ordination between administrative activities and popular will together with co-operations. It becomes all the more important, he felt that the administrator has his finger on the pulse of the people all the time, and the people feel that he is one of them that he is reflecting their wishes and will always continue to do so.[29]

In the ultimate analysis, Nehru aims both at the growth of the individual as well as of the state. Freedom of the individual is as necessary on the freedom of the state for such growth. Finally freedom itself leads to a higher ideal.

"Freedom for a nation and a people may be, and as I believe always good in the long run, but in the final analysis freedom itself is a means to an end, that end being the raising of the people in question to higher levels and hence the general advancement of humanity."[30]

Public Sector and Industrial Policy 1948

The industrial policy resolution of April 1948 under the leadership of first Prime Minister Jawaharlal Nehru of Independent India was the true example of his basic ideas of public sector which contempleted a mixed economy reserving a sphere for the private sector and another for public sector. In this policy category first, second and third were related to private sector where as fourth category was left to private sector.

But in the Industrial Policy Resolution, 1956 the so called 'Industrial Constitution of India' was properly drafted by Jawaharlal Nehru in which schedule A & B was placed with public sector and 'D' was left to private sector.

Industrial Policy Resolution 1956 and Public Sector

The 1956 Industrial Policy Resolution was described as the economic constitution based on its political counterpart the constitution of India. It stated clearly the inherent right of the state to acquire any industrial undertaking. It expressed doubts in the ability of the private sector by itself, to bring about fast economic development. The dice was heavily loaded in favour of public sector. The private sector got less consideration. "The so-called private sector became a sort of residuary legatee. Economic development was more explicitly equated with State enterprise."[32] There was a general fear that the public sector would grow into a giant mainly to grab the private sector. The fear was based on misreading of the Resolution. The Policy statement secured for private sector a permanent plac in the economy. The public sector was not to develop as a rival but create congenial condition and an infrastructure which would facilitate the growth of private sector.

The Resolution, however, left ample scope for the expansion of the private sector as well. D.K. Rangnekar rightly comments "The Industrial Policy Resolution of 1958 set out some of the principles of Nehru's philosophy though it retained sufficient anbivalence to placate the uncommitted elements."[33]

Prime Minister Nehru saw through the game of foreign capital and multinationals and pushed through a programme of public sector steel plants. There is no doub that this policy resulted to rapid expansion of the public sector in basic and heavy industries but as Rangnekar has rightly put it, "private sector investment zoomed in the wake of public sector expansion."

Thus according to Nehru after the attainment of independence and advent of planning, there has been a progressive expansion is the scope of public sector. The passage of Industrial policy Resolution of 1956 and the adoption of the socialistic pattern of society as our national goal further led to a deliberate enlargement of the role of public sector. To understand the role of public sector, we must have an idea should its size in the context of the Indian economy. For a comprehensive view of the entire public sector, we should cover besides autonomous corporations, the departmental enterprises while doing so, not only the enterprises owned and run by the central government be covered but the enterprises run by the state government, be covered but the enterprise run by the State Government and local bodies should also be included. Secondly, it would not be appropriate to use any single measure to estimate the size of public sector, rather it would be desirable to use quite a few indicators e.g. employment, investment, value of output, national income generated saving, capital formation and capital stock.

Accountability of Public Sector and Nehru

Besides, he also clearly defined the accountability and autonomy of public sector. To him, problem of accountability in public sector has, perhaps been one of the most important aspects. He called accountability as a king pin of democratic administration. Accountability is real to the extent that the legislature is able to perceive and scrutinize the activities of public sector and thereby to satisfy itself that public policies remain and thereby to satisfy itself that public policies remain opposite to the needs and aspirations of the people and that the programmes of the public sector and efficiently implemented.

Nehru made it clear that public sector units are the creation of the government and are placed in the hands of Boards of Directors for implementation of the development and industrial tasks envisaged the government. Thus, the government being the only or the merit, important shareholder, expects accountability from the management in order to satisfy itself that the public investments are safe and productive and that the objectives are being realised.

It is obvious from the views of Nehru that public sector should be accountable to parliament, the true representative of the public and the tax payers without at the same time affecting their autonomy and subjecting them in public criticism on the floor of the House.

Principles of Accountability

Nehru stated the following principles of accountability[35] that it —

(a) needs more doers than watchers;

(b) must be defined clearly;

(c) is multiway process;

(d) is one's capacity to account;

(e) is limited by capacity

(f) requires it modes; and

(g) is quality controlled process

Nehru as such played very significant role in defining:

(a) parliamentary accountability

(b) ministerial accountability; and

(c) audit accountability in term of public sector undertaking.

He was the true pleader of maintainign balance between accountability and autonomy for their rapid, balanced and accelerated growth. Since the days of Nehru Public Sector Undertakings as a model employer, have continued to recognize and render their social responsibilities towards welfare of employees of Public Sector Enterprises. Even in the open economic market scenairo, public enterprises have made their significant contributions by providing necessary facilities for the projects located in green field areas and away from existing towns and villages in inaccessible areas in the time with the country's source economic goals.

REFERENCES

1. Nehru Jawaharlal, *An Autobiography*, IV 25 noted from Das, M.N., *The Political Philosophy of Jawaharlal Nehru*, George Allen & Unwin, London, 1961, p. 24.

2. *Ibid., An Autobiography*, Vol. V; p. 35.

3. *Ibid.*

4. *Ibid.*
5. *Ibid.*
6. Das, M.N., *op. cit.*, pp. 124-125.
7. *An Autobiography*, XLVI, p. 361.
8. *Ibid.*
9. *Ibid.*, pp. 362-63.
10. Das, M.N., *op. cit.*, p. 127.
11. Nehru Jawaharlal, *The Discovery of India*, Vol. II, p. 280.
12. *Ibid.*
13. *Ibid.*, Vol. VII, p. 127, Containing Bentonon's Quotation.
14. Das M.N., *op. cit.*, pp. 127-128.
15. Nehru Jawaharlal, *The Discovery of India, op. cit.*, p. 282.
16. Do, *An Autobiography*, Vol. VIII, p. 42, *op. cit.*
17. Das, M.N., *op. cit.*, p. 129.
18. Nehru Jawaharlal, *The Discovery of India, op. cit.*, p. 335.
19. Do, *An Autobiography, op. cit.*, XXVI, 182.
20. Do, Essay II - 27, *Parliamentary Address*, December 1929.
21. Nehru Jawaharlal, *Writing*, II Part II, Chapter 3, p. 72.
22. Sitarammaiya Pattabhi, *The History of Indian National Congress*, 1885-1935, p. 782, Lok Sabha Secretariate, New Delhi.
23. Deo, Narendra Narain, Jay Prakash & Patwardhan, Achuty, *Ibid*.
24. Nehru Jawaharlal, Essay II, 82-83, Presidential Address 5, April 1936.
25. Do, *Writings* 1, 339-40.
26. Do, Speeches 1, 6 August 15, 1947, *Broadcast to the Nation*.
27. *Public Enterprises Survey* 2002-03, Vol. I, p. 189, Government of India, Bureau of Public Enterprises.

5

Nehru on Indian Planning

Introduction

Planning is the process of preparing a blueprint of action to attain stated objectives within the time frame. The determination of objectives, the specification of targets, the strategy for mobilisation of resources, the allocation of outlays to different development sectors, the blueprint of action (including their operationalisation in the shape of policies programmes and their delivery system) are aspects which have to be considered in any planning exercise according to Pt. Jawaharlal Nehru.

Concept of Planning & Nehru

The concept of economic planning has attracted the attention of economists, statesmen, social reformers and scientists in modern times.[1] To him, planning is a method, a technique or a means to an end, the end being the realisation of social objectives set by bodies representatives of the nation. According to Nehru, under economic planning there are some specific ends to be achieved. In planning there must have clear objectives. These objectives are governed by certain social imperative, planning simply means that we make, well thought out approach to solve our problems.[2] He argued that planning is a scientific approach to the national problems that face us not leaving it just to chance. It is, essentially, a scientific approach to the problems of life and nation that constitute planning. The planning must have an ideal before its' some kind of an objective, a social objective not a rigid one.

Moreover, planning is a "logical, scientific and organised approach to an objective."[3] Jawaharlal Nehru strongly argued that planning is essential because it enables us to formulate with some precision what we intend to achieve within a given time frame.

He stated, "planning is something like ladder by which you go from one step of development to another step of development and ultimately to the better and brighter goal.[4] To him, planning is only a system of organisation of all activities production, distribution and consumption and their proper co-ordination. In other words, planning means laying down a scheme of a planned economy for the nation comprising all its activities, under their proper co-ordination for the common good."[5]

Economic planning means securing a better balance between demand and supply by a conscious and well thought out plan or control of production and distribution. It may be called a technique of balances on which success of planning can only be determined. In a more homely way he tried to define "planning is a kind of house keeping" for the nation.[6]

In his own words, "But the moment the scientist or technologist comes on the scene, be he Russian or American, the conclusion are the same for the simple reason that planning and development today are almost a matter of mathematics."[7]

The approach of Nehru was pragmatic and practical. Planning is a continuous movement towards desired goals and objectives. The principal agencies which decide the plan and implement it must have knowledge about what it is planning for and to whom and some picture of future also. Planning is done by central authority.

Nehru As a Planner

Nehru was a planner long before he got the authority which could enable him to introduce planning in Indian economy. He had an immense faith in planning. He had very clear ideas about its significance, its objectives and strategy.

His faith in planning is considered anti-dated Indian independence and to many people it is surprising that Nehru's idea of planned economic development was not given formal shape until 1951 when first five year plan was inaugurated by him. Thus, despite his enthusiasm and faith, it was not until 1950 that a planning commission with himself as Chairman was established to formulate to appraise and to examine the Indian Planning.

Economic Planning & Nehru

He had long been personally interested in economic planning having been much impressed by what he saw during his visit to Soviet Russia in 1927. Inspired by the Soviet economic experiment, Nehru found economic planning as the only panaces for social political and economic ills of the developing and under developed countries of the world.

Russian Planning & Nehru

He deeply studied the Soviet Russian economic planning in addition to Indian. The Soviet Second Five Year Plan, which began in 1929, impressed Nehru much. Nehru was drawn towards economic planning. Russian achievement of economic development through economic planning had influenced his mind and heart alike.[8] He further observed that problems of Russia and India and other under developed countries were considered identical.

Much earlier in 1934, M. Visveswaraya had published a Ten Year Plan aimed at doubling the national income.

He was fully convinced that Russia experiments might

help India in finding out a solution for her socio-economic problems.[9] In this connection National Planning Committee was constituted, in 1938 headed by Nehru himself at the instance of National Congress. It produced a series of reports and plans of various kinds which today serve for no more than historical interest. Soon after formulation of well known "Bombay Plan" in 1944 the idea of planned economy received a fillip. Bombay plan was prepared and published under the signature of dozen or so well known Indian industrialists and business leaders like J.R.D. Tata, G.D. Birla, Sir Hori Modi, N.R. Sarkar and others. According to him Bombay plan was regarded as being crucial for sustaining, self-growth, self-generating and satisfactory growth of the economy.[10]

Planning Advisory Board

Nehru immediately set up a Planning Advisory Board as soon as the interim government came into the picture in 1946. He formed an economic programme committee of the Congress with himself as chairman which submitted its report in 1948. The Planning Commission was constituted in 1950 on the basis of this report.

Relevance

Obviously Nehru was plan-minded and as such, Planning Commission is the greatest gift of Nehru to the prosperity of India. He advocated that Planning Commission, is an advisory agency nothing more. But its advices carry great weight as it is an expert body. To quote him," I think that first of all a planning commission is absolutely essential we can't move without it, and if any government tries to move without it, it will come to trouble.[12] During his regime three five year plans were launched.

He made it clear that in order to progress we must save money for investment for further progress every year. We must produce more than we consume. We have to face demands a carefully planned and scientific approach as to utilise our available resources in the best possible way. We have to avoid upsetting and wastage of rare resources. Consequently he repeatedly stressed the need of proper and maximum utilisation of our resources. We have to go to the roots of these problems and this involves attaching the evil as it is. Furthermore, planning is essential for balanced economic development of the country.

He stated, "plannign essentially consists in balancing the balance between industry and agriculture, between heavy and light industry and cottage and other industries."[14]

Planning & Jawaharlal Nehru after Independence

According to Jawaharlal Nehru The 'Directive Principles of State Policy' enstrined in our constitution though, not enforceable by any court, lay down principles fundamental to the governance of the country.

Article 37 of Indian Constitution clearly states that it will be the duty of the state to apply these principles in making laws. In this context Articles 38, 39. 39A, 40, 41, 43, 46, 47, 48 and 48A are more important articles.[15] Consisting of promotion of welfare of the people ensuring adequate means of livelihood for its citizens, protection of interests of children and women, organising village panchayats, right to work, to education, to public assistance in some educational and economic interests of the weaker sections of society, standard of living protection and improvement of environment and safeguarding of forests and wild life etc.

The constitution contains provisions relating to the broad directions to be followed by the state is relation to the welfare and development of people of the country.

Planning Commission: Composition, Powers and Functions

Jawaharlal Nehru played key role is setting up a

technical body like planning commission for facilitating the planning process in our country. It was set up in March 1950. Nehru stated the following functions of the planning commission.[16]

(i) To make an assessment of the material capital and human resources of the country, including technical personnel and investigate the possibilities of augmenting such of the resources as are found to be deficient is relation to the nations's requirements.

(ii) To formulate a plan for the most effective and balanced utilisation of the country's resources.

(iii) To determine priorities, define the stages in which the plan should be carried out and purpose the allocation of resources for the one completion of each stage.

(iv) To indicate the factors which tend to retard economic development and determine the conditions which, in view of the current social, political and economic situation, should be created for the successful execution of the plan.

(v) To determinate the nature of the machinery which will be necessary for securing the successful implementations of each stage of the plan in all its aspects.

(vi) To appraise from time to time the progress achieved in the execution of each stage of the plan and recommend the adjustments of policy and measures that such appraisal may should to be necessary and

(vii) To make such interim or ancilliary recommendations as appear to be appropriate either for facilitating the discharge of the duties assigned to it or on a consideration of prevailing economic conditions, current policies, measures and development pogrammes or on an examination of such specific problems as may be referred to it for advice by central and state governments.

Organisation of Planning Commission

The organisationof the Planning Commission facilitates its role as an advisory body functioning at the highest policy level without further being involved in the responsibilities of day to day administration.

The Prime Minister is the chairman of the planning commission. The commission has a Deputy Chairman and six or more full time members. The Finance Minister and a few other Ministers of Cabinet rank are ex-officio members. At times, the Depty Chairman is also the Minister of Planning. A full time secretary co-ordinates the technical and administrative activities.

Various Divisions of Planning Commissions

The planning commission functions through a series of divisions and sections. According to Nehru it has eight general divisions and eighteen subject divisions.

A. General Divisions

(a) Economic Divisions;

(i) Finance Resource Division;

(ii) Development Policy Division;

(iii) International Economics Division;

(iv) Socio-Economic Research Unit;

(b) Perspective Planning Division;

(c) Labour, Employment and Manpower Division;

(d) Statistics and Survey Division;

(e) State Plans Divisions, including Multi-level Planning; area Development and North-Eastern Regions;

(f) Project Appraisal Divison;

(g) Monitoring and Information Divison;

(h) Plan co-ordination Division;

B. Subject Divisions

(a) Science and Technology Division;

(b) Agriculture Divisions;

(c) Rural Development Division;

(d) Rrrigation and Command Area Development Division;

(e) Power and Energy Division;

(f) Industry and Minerals Division;

(g) Village and Small Industries Division;

(h) Transport Division;

(i) Education Division;

(j) Rural Energy Division;

(k) Housing urban Development and Water Supply Division;

(l) Health and Family Welfare Division;

(m) Social Welfare Division;

(n) Backward class Division;

(o) Communication and Information Division;

(p) Indo-Japan Committee;

(q) Computer Service Division;

(r) Western Ghats Secretariat;

Within the general organisation of the Planning Commission, the Programme Evaluation Organisation (PEO) has functioned since 1952 as an ancilliary agency. It undertakes evaluation studies to assess the impact of selected plan programmes in order to provide feedback to the planners and implementing agencies.

Jawaharlal Nehru is regarded as the architect of planning in India. He viewed planning as a way of developing the country avoiding the unnecessary rigours of an industrial transition in so far as it affected the lives of the masses living in India's villages. Moreover, he recognised that planning was a positive instrument for resolving imbalances and contradiction in a large and hetrogeneous country such as India.

National Development Council

According to Nehru the National Development Council (NDC) in the highest policy making body which provides the opportunity for plans to be formulated and implemented throughout the country as a unified development effort. Prime Minister is the chairman of NDC. Its members comprise Cabinet Ministers (some not all) Chief Ministers of all the States and Members of the Planning Commission. The NDC is the body at the highest policy making level which approves the approach and latter the final plan.

Planning Units of Central Ministries

Since the Central Ministries have a very important role in the formulation of plans and considerable state in the policies and programmes which ultimately find a place, most central ministries have separate divisions or units for co-ordination the work of the ministry concerned to undertake these functions. The planning unit works in close collaboration with programme division. It also initiates and co-ordinates the work of the working group that are set up for preparing the plan. The draft proposals incorporating the suggestions of the different working groups are also prepared by it and these are then finalised by the Department/Ministry concerned and sent to the Planning Commission.

As in the centre, so also in the states, a number of organisations and departments are involved in the planning process.

Multi Level Planning

Decentralised planning for rural development, according to Nehru should be viewed in relation to various levels and agencies operating to influence development. Decentralised planning is defined as that form of planning where the task of formulating, adopting, executing and supervising the plan is dispersed, rather than entrusted to a central authority. In decentralised planning the regional bodies and local enterprises are given greater freedom to formulate, adopt and implement the plan.

Nehru rightly advocated that centralisation or decentralisation are not by themselves good or bad. Both these methods of planning derive their character from the political and administrative structure, political philosophy, past practice, public pressures and other factors.

In India, planning is decentralised to some extent since the states have definite responsibilities. The need for decentralised planning provides the justification for planning at multiple level. The former provides the logic for the existence of the latter. Decentralised planning process makes planning more meaningful, democratic and responsive to the needs of those for whom planning is meant. Multi-level planning implies identification of levels at which planning functions are assigned and the respective areas of responsibilities. Multilevel planning, thus, leads to decentralisation of planning functions.

The idea of decentralised planning has been familiar to planners for a long time. A multi-level structure of planning for the country based on the politico-administrative structure is shown in following chart.

Chart I

Planning level	*Political/ Administrative Terrotorict Equivalent*	*Abstract Territorial Equivalent*	*Planning Concept*
Macro-Level (National Plan)	Nation		Central Planning/ Policy Planning Sectoral Planning
Meso - Level (Sub-national) Budgetary Plan	State	State/Resource Region/River	State Plan/ Sectoral Planning
Plan or State Plan)		Valley/Metro-politan Region	Regional Planning/Town & Country Planning.
Macro - Level (Decentralised Development Plan)	District	Area	District Planning/ Area
	Block	Sub-area/ micro-region	Micro-level planning/Block level Planning
	Village	local level	village Production plan and Planning for Target Group

The focus of development planning is on transforming the rural areas keeping the social, economic, technological and cultural horizons in mind. The plan at lower level should save the freedom to choose among national objectives for the following reasons.

(a) feasibility or relevance

(b) freedom to fix priorities

(c) target fixing

(d) information base

(e) relationship among plan objectives.

Organisation Powers and Functions of District Planning

Jawaharlal Nehru was the prime supporter of district planning in India. In his views district planning is a kind of area-based sub-state planning and arises from the need to supplement the national and state plans with a more detailed examination of the resources, problems and potentials of local areas so that investment programmes more specifically tailored to the particular needs of district could be evolved and implemented.

District planning can't be viewed in isolation from either the state plan or the block plan, the latter being another area-based plan at a lower administrative level. The scope of the district plan should be open ended in recognition of the linkages available beyond and district.

District Planning Needs to Consider Three Points

(i) regional affinities in tune with natural geographical regions covering more than one district.

(ii) recognition of sub-regional elements within a district.

(iii) building up of capacity, authority and skills at local institutions.

District planning should keep the national and state objectives in view, in so far as such objectives can be conceived in the broad background of a district.

Components of District Planning

Jawaharlal Nehru elucidated following components of District Planning.

A. Spatial component

B. Economic component

C. Social component

D. Administrative component

A. Spatial Component

Spatial component is very important comprehensive. Spatial plan would need to consider the physical resources, land use and all human settlements in a region right from the smallest settlement to the city. The district plan needs to identify and correct imbalances in infrastructural facilities in the district as a whole or in any part of it. It needs also to consider the elements of sub-regionalisations should consider the linkages, both economic and social among a group of settlements, based on the principle of functional interdependence, e.g. around markets, trading centres, or areas served by specialised health services. The pattern of physical distribution of infrastrucure and service facilities would determine the nature of interdependence. It is necessary that spatial characteristics and norms should be considered.

B. Economic Component

Nehru made it clear that economic planning had traditionally been the core of planning, since a principal aim of development planning had been to increase income and employment. According to him economic component consists of

- resources
- agro-economic features
- socio-economic factors
- infrastructural features
- sectoral profiles; etc.

Economic planning, in additon would, require knowledge about geological, ground-water, forest, soil, human and other resources available.

Economic planning in the district needs to be made in the context of available financial resources such as:

(a) resources available the state and the centre for particular projects in the district;

(b) resources available from state and the central for schemes of general nature not tied to specific projects:

(c) resources from non-government and voluntary agencies.

C. Social Component

Nehru also explained that a district plan can't afford to overlook the social component of planning. The task of a district planning according to Nehru, is also to reduce social inequalities, provide social services and ensure public participation. For district plan, public participation is both an important tool and a goal for development since planning is the medium of social transformation and means to bridge the gap between the government and the people. As such, people's participation in planning is necessary.

D. Administrative Component

Regarding administrative component he advocated that the success or failure of district planning in ultimately influenced by political and administrative set-up of the district planning machinery. The Collector/District Magistrate is at the administrative apex of the district. He is supported by the District Planning Boards/Committee.

The chairman of the planning committee may be a Minister, Member of Parliament, M.L.A. or District Collector.

The Planning machinery at district level may be illustrated from following chart-II.

Chart II

Apex Planning at District Level	*States having this type of Body*
1. District Planning Board Meghalaya, Nagaland,	Gujarat, Madhya Pradesh, Punjab.
2. District Planning Committee	Rajasthan, Manipur, Sikkim.
3. Zila Parishad	West Bengal, Karnataka.
4. Zila Development Board	Andhra Pradesh
5. District Development Committee	Himachal Pradesh, Assam
6. District Development Committee	J&K Orissa
7. District Development Council	Kerala, Tamil Nadu
8. District Planning & Development Council	Bihar, Maharashtra
9. District Planning & Monitoring Committee	U.P.

Pre Condition of District Planning

Moreover, according to Nehru district planning in India requires following attempt for building up of:

- Political will and commitment;
- Setting up of District Planning Body in each district;
- Clear demarcations of Planning functions;
- Training and personnel;
- Evolution of new patterns of political and administrative patterns of functioning;
- Setting up a suitable machinery for planning in each district;
- Delegation of administrative powers;

- Ensure public participation at all stages of planning process;
- Working art criteria for inter district allocation of outlays;
- Disaggregation of plan funds and devolution of financial resources.

Pre-planning Phase of District Planning

Before embarking up on a district plan, the steps, according to Nehru, at the pre-planning stage are as follows:

(a) defining the scope and content of a district plan;

(b) disaggregation of plan funds from the state to district level on appropriate criteria;

(c) establishing a district planning unit at the state level;

(d) affecting certain administrative decentralisation measures;

(e) making arrangements for the training of personnel; and,

(f) establishing a proper district planning machinery.

It is necessary to ensure adequate administrative decentralisation at pre-planning stage itself. Within the framework of decentralised multi-level planning, the district planning authority needs to:

- Identify local needs and objectives within the given national and state level objectives;
- List the natural and human resources in the district and level of development attained so far, also at sub-regional levels;
- formulate district plan;

- Co-ordinate implementation of district plan and
- Monitor and review the implementation of district plan.

Components of Planning Phase

In the planning phase, according to Nehru, following steps are involved:

(a) formulation of the major objectives of the district plans;

(b) compilation of data for district planning;

(c) preparing the profile of the district in relation to the basic objectives;

(d) formulating the main strategy and thrust of district planning and;

(e) analysis of existing programmes and projects with reference to the strategy outlined. This implies;

(i) modification of ongoing programmes and projects;

(ii) proposals for removal of inter block disparities;

(iii) indication of relationship and links between the district plan and regional and state development plans;

(iv) assessment of resources for allocation to various programmes and projects;

(v) inclusion of new projects and plans;

(vi) statement of spatial dimensions of the district plan;

(vii) a statement of physical and financial components of the district plan and;

(viii) organisation and management to ensure that no implementation gap exist;

Nehru and Financial and Physical Planning

Physicall planning refers to the allocation of physical resources i.e. real resources such as labour, machinery, raw materials, etc. While financial planning implies planning in terms of money. It has rightly been felt by Jawaharlal Nehru that an efficient machinery of economic planning should first acquire the ability to build up a set of targets which are mutually consistent.[17]

"Let us think also of the mighty resources of India which, if harnessed and utilised for the common good, can change the face of India and make her great and prosperous."[18]

In fact, finance is only a camp-follower and a mobiliser of real physical resources. He said that physical approach to planning was more important for under-developed economy. He observed "I myself do not see any other way of rapid progress. The financial approach to planning is not rapid enough."[19]

Nehru had a scant view about the financial approach to economic planning. He did not want finance to limit physical needs or targets of the plan. He considered finance as secondary and physical as prime consideration.

He was quite obvious that planning will always be perspective planning and as such physical and financial planning both are intimately related. Both have to be considered.

Democratic Planning and Nehru

Nehru had a deep attachment to the values of freedom,

democracy, socialism and the welfare of the common citizen. He had unquestioning faith in the creative dynamic stregth of democracy. In a democratic country like India, we cannot think of any social objective which does not touch the vast masses of the people of India. If we do not keep these social objectives alive, the socio-planning structure cracks up. Nehru adopted this method of democratic planning, because for him it is only system which will function properly in India, on the countrary any other system will have harmful effects. To Nehru democratic planning means the utilization of all our available resources and, in particular, the maximum quantity of labour willingly given and rightly directed so as to promote the good of the community and the individual.[20] Planning Commission with Nehru as its Chairman was set up under democratic planning. He had tried his best to link up the working of planning commission directly with the fundamental rights and the Directive Principles of State Policy embodied in the Indian Constitution. Our country is of federal structure. Consequently, he advocated democratic planning in India.[21]

Flexible and Rigid Planning & Nehru

Planning is a "panacea" of our entire socio-economic ills. But, Nehru stated, "if you make a thing rigid and permanent, you stop a nation's growth, the growth of a living, vital, organic people.[22] He was of the opinion that planning does not, and should not possess any dogmatic element about the future. Planning may not always be quote accurate and final and rigid because socio-economic conditions vary day after day month after month and year - after year. Even parliament cannot, by only law, lay down how whole population of our country will work. We cannot force them to do something, at any rate in a democratic system of government. It may be possible in authoritarian and totalitarian form of government.[23]

As such, there can be no finality or rigidity about such a plan. It must be flexible as the plan progresses, there are new developments, new experiences and new trends.[24] Thus, intelligent development plans should be subject to revisions in the light of new experiences. A plan must always be subject to revision if it is to be kept up-to-date. Two things are necessary:

(a) long term planning

(b) planning for relatively shorter periods.

According to him, a fixed planning is not only worthless but dangerous to the nation. There should be certain flexibility.[25]

Nehru and Perspective Planning

Nehru regarded planning as "a continuous process,"[26] as a flow stream because only then there will be a rhythm of expansion in the development of the country. The idea of a time a period is implicit and inherent in the very concept of planning.

For Nehru indeed, perspective planning is of the essence of the planning process today. Even in considering a five year period,[27] perspective and long term planning has always to be kept in view. A perspective plan is a blue print of development to be undertaken over a longer period. In his own words, "therefore, planning means perspective planning."[28]

But the real importance of all this lies in its being a base for future progress. According to Nehru perspective planning takes into account the growth of population, technology, education, power resources, machine in building industries etc. he constituted a perspective planning division within Indian planning. The perspective planning is of great importance requiring the active co-operation of demographers, economists, statisticians, engineers, technicians. Scientists etc. and there aspects of long term growth of the national economy as a whole. He as such supported perspected planning. He was ready to sacrify today in the hope that the future will be better and bright, he said we work not only for today but much more for tomorrow we build for the future.[29] He thus suggested for long term and short term perspective planning.

Balanced Planning and Nehru

To Nehru, it is necessary to draw up the various balances even before. The final production targets or schedules in important branches of the national economy are laid down.[30] He advocated the idea of balanced planning. According to him in a state economy, some kind of balance can be achieved at the cost of poverty and the starvation of the people. But in the economy of a developing economy, one has to take care at every step least one step create difficulties.[31]

Nehru was of the opinion that there will be no industrial growth unless machines are made here, unless iron and steel are manufactured here. Unless we balance the heavy industry with the growth of village industry, we shall produce an unbalanced structure of economy which may crack up and fall to pieces. Thus, the importance of village industry, household industry, cottage industry and small scale industry is very great. It is great from the point of view of employment generation, production of consumer goods. Planning essentially consists of balancing between industry and agriculture, heavy and light industry, cottage and other industries and between urban and rural. A development plan should possess regional balance. Thus, according to him balanced regional development is highly essential in Indian Planning.

Human Aspects in Planning and Nehru

Human aspect was regarded as an important aspect of planning by Nehru. As he says, the financial aspect is important but is far less important than the human aspect.[32] In his opinion, the human factor is the basic and most important factor in any work to be done. He after all, accepted that main thing is the human being, and not what plants or factories we put up. Thus, the human factor has always to kept in mind, the growth of human being and all our social, scientific things should be governed by this consideration.[33] Merely a higher standard of material comforts can't be the main criterian for measuring the real progress+blank nation. He observed that "It is the development of the human being and human personality that count.[34] It is recognised that "investment in man" is much more important than "material investment."[35]

It is therefore, quite evident that even for success of planned economic development in the normal sense of the term, it is absolutely essential to develop the inner qualities of new man and women constituting the community or the nation as a whole. According to Nehru, "planning involves very important aspects; i.e. human aspect consisting of education, training, morale, character, skills, population discipline, health, medical facilities, motivation etc.

REFERENCES

1. *Selected Work of Jawaharlal Nehru, op. cit.*, 1977, p. 516.
2. *Ibid.*, Vol. III, 1972, p. 250.
3. *Speeches of Jawaharlal Nehru*, Vol. V, 1968, p. 147.
4. *Ibid.*, p. 70.
5. *Ibid.*, p. 81.
6. *Selected Works of Jawaharlal Nehru*, Vol. IX, 1976, p. 399.
7. *Speeches of Nehru, op. cit.*, Vol. II, 1967, p. 75.
8. *Interview*, R.K. Karanjia, 1960, pp. 50-51.
9. Nehru, Jawaharlal, *Glimpses of World History*, 1949, p. 939.
10. Nehru, Jawaharlal, *Soviet Russia*, 1928, p. 4.
11. *Speeches of Nehru*, Vol. V, *op. cit.*, 1968, p. 124, Lok Sabha Secretariat, New Delhi.
12. *Ibid.*, Vol. II, 1967, p. 121.

13. *Ibid.*, p. 129.
14. *Selected Works of Jawaharlal Nehru*, Vol. X, 1977, p. 520.
15. *Constitution of India*, Articles 38, 39, 40, 41, 43, 46, 47, 48 Govt. of India, New Delhi.
16. *Planning Commission*, Govt. of India, New Delhi, Ist Five Year Plan.
17. *Speeches of Jawaharlal Nehru*, Vol. IV, 1964, p. 123.
18. *Ibid.*, Vol. I, 1967, p. 83.
19. *Ibid.*, Vol. III, 1970, p. 20.
20. *Ibid.*, Vol. II, 1967, p. 94.
21. *Ibid.*, Vol. IV, 1963, p. 126.
22. *Speeches of Jawaharlal Nehru*, Vol. II, 1967, p. 40.
23. *Ibid.*, Vol. V, 1968, p. 81.
24. *Ibid.*, Vol. III, 1970, p. 21.
25. *Ibid.*, Vol. III, 1970, p. 77.
26. *Ibid.*, Vol. III, 1970, p. 91.
27. *Ibid.*
28. *Ibid.*, Vol. IV, 1964, pp. 134-35.
29. *Ibid.*, Vol. II, 1967, p. 535.
30. *Glimpses of World History*, J. Nehru, 1949, p. 854.
31. *Speeches of Jawaharlal Nehru*, Vol. III, 1970, p. 51.
32. *Ibid.*, Vol. IV, 1964, p. 148.
33. *Ibid.*, p. 147.
34. *Ibid.*, Vol. IV, 1964, p. 147.
35. *Ibid.*

6

Nehru on Parliament

Introduction

The purpose of this chapter is to attempt for filling a gap in the field of studies of Nehru as a parliamentarian. For his unique role in building the great institution of Parliament and establishing loftly parliamentary traditions, conventions and procedures had not received due attention from schoars. The present chapter projects the views of Jawaharlal Nehru contributed to parliamentary democracy. As a democratic thinker, he emerges unparallel. As a framer of our constitution, he appears most articulate in expounding its philosophy and in giving concrete shape to its democratic content. He obviously shines as a parliamentarian as the ideal one worthy of emolation. His conduct in the house, be it during the discussions of question hour, his treatment with opposition, his attitude to criticism, his respect and regard for the chair and overall the time and energy he devoted to parliamentary work all bear eloquent testimony to his greatness as a parliamentarian.

Nehru as an Architect of Modern Parliamentary Democracy

Pandit Jawaharlal Nehru was the prime artificer of modern India and of her system of representative parliamentary democracy. His contribution to the evolution of India's political system was unique. It was Nehru who built brick by brick the infrastructure and the edifice of the institution, called the Parliament of India. He has an abriding faith in the parliamentary system because for him it meant a government by consultation and discussion and, as such a responsible and responsive government.

Himself an erudite scholar and a reputed author, Pandit Jawaharlal Nehru inspired many intellectuals and academics Volumes have been written on him, on his life and works, his Prime Ministership, his foreign policy and more recently on his active role in Constitution-making.[1] Unfortunately, however, very little research seems to have been undertaken so far on his role in building up the great institution of Parliament tradition, conventions and procedures.

Faith in Parliamentary Democracy

Nehru with his abounding faith in democracy devotedly attempted to develop all the parliamentary institutions. While he lived, he was a practaising democrat. He even tried to democratise the nation with a three tier administration, unique, state and Panchayat. Subsequently to his pasting away, the entire system under unimaginative leadership whose only objective was more power in their own hands, successfully demolished the time concept of the three tier administration which could have ushered in the government of the people. The skeleton is still their but without flesh and blood or any sembalance of dynamics, the poor farmer, artisan and the masses are still ruled as of old under the colonial system.[2]

Nehru desired that Parliament should consists of capable, independent and right thinking men and women who would offer their opnions freely whenever so demanded without fear and favour. He brought great regards to the parliamentarians by giving respect to the institution of Parliament itself. He always held that speaker of either house of Parliament, once elected to the high office, must hold scale even between member and member. He despised weakness in any presiding officer when he came to know that such an officer is in the queue for some favours or patronage from the ruling clique.[3]

Opposition in Parliament and Nehru

Nehru deliberately gave great attention to the opposition in the Parliament because it was quite weak. The Kamraj Plan drafted by Mr. Biju Patnaik and approved by Nehru was read out in the Jaipur Session of Congress contained a paragraph.

"It is the duty of the Congress Party as the only national party of India usher in a two party system with strong foundations without which the democratic conventions and institutions of today are bound to go into decay within foreseable future."[4]

Nehru insisted that executive must be accountable to the Parliament. Thus, all the House Committees should be given weightage by the executive and the report of these committees received due considerations in the Parliament, only because Nehru liked it.

Nehru as a True Democrat

An independent, sovereign democratic republic was Jawaharlal Nehru's dream much before destiny called upon him to handle the affairs of the state as India's first Prime Minister.

Nehru was first of our socialists, yet he believed in the socialist ideal as a form of action, not as a dogma.[5] In his scheme of things, democracy was inter-woven with socialism for him planning was an economic imperative to lend contact and meaning to democracy as a political concept. Individual freedom as a concept had become part of the great illusion with the rise of capitalism.

Existing Models

Thus, in the purely modernistic context of which Nehru was doubtless a representative figure, the democratic system for free India could not be an imitation of the existing models in the west.

He was a democrat as well as a socialist and this combination booked strange to many as observer. For him, the two roles were not contradictory but complementary to each other.

The founding father of our constitution had two outstanding models of democracy before them. But India had to adopt her own pattern of democracy without being an imitation or even a mixture of any particular system. In his Independence Day Speech from the ramparts of the Red Fort in 1949, Nehru had this to tell the nation.

"Our constituent assembly is busy framing a new Constitution for India and soon we shall adopt a republican form of government. However, laws and constitutions do not by themselves make a country great. It is the enthusiasm, energy and constant efforts of a people that make it a great nation, men of law lay down constitution but history is really made by great minds, large hearts and stont arms; by the sweet, tears and tail of a people."[6]

Both as a visionary and a statesman, Nehru viewed this process in the spirit of what he called the Indian revolution and the country's economic and political imperatives. To Dr. S. Radhakrishna, "Nehru is essentially a democrat. In his way of thinking there is no place for intolerance, racial or social condescension or national aggressiveness. Even when he acquiesces in policies, that are not quite consistent with the spirit of democracy he does so with the utmost reluctance. In an infant democracy like ours, he is anxious that we should not, set up wrong precedents."[7]

Master Builder of Parliamentary Democracy

Jawaharlal Nehru was indeed master builder, one of the few architects in the delicate and uncommon art of national building. But he was not an isolated creation. He was the product of half a century or freedom struggle and moulded by men like Gandhiji.

It is stated that man is the centre of universe. Almost in the same vein Jawaharlal Nehru declared that the centre of democratic process was the individual himself. Nehru gave primary to the individual was the product of and conditioned by socio-economic organisation in which he lived. The individual and society were inter-dependent and not exclusive entitles. His arguments, simple, elegant straight forward as they were embody some of the foundational philosophical premises democracy. He once observed.

"We have definitely accepted the democratic process."[8] Democracy is a means to an end."[9] Nehru knew too well that parliamentary democracy was not something which could be created ina country by some majic word. It had to evolve and grow. It had to be imbided. He gave reasons for the government and opting certain measures and explain to them various points through his speeches and addresses both inside and outside the Parliament. He almost took upon himself the role of an educator of the people. He also wanted that policies and programmes of the government were properly debated, understood, evaluated and accepted. To him democracy was the best form of government. He asserted that in a democratic polity, individual was offered the fullest opportunity for self development as well as to do good to society, democracy promoted the virtues of self discipline and a sense of social responsibility. Its methods and objective were peaceful and it followed the dictum that right means lead to right ends. He strongly argued.

"We believe in democracy. It is the right means to

achieve ends and because it is a peaceful method. It removes the pressure which other forms of government may impose on the individual. It transforms the discipline which is imposed by authority largely to self discipline. A social organisation must have some discipline to hold it together. In a proper democracy discipline is self imposed. There is no democracy if there is no discipline."[10] He further advocated that democracy had the ability to move the masses and to involve them through their free will in the task of development, national building and social progress. The Government remains responsible to the people and is ever responsive to their wishes and demand. Through parliament, an intimate relationship is forged between Government and the people.

It is a well recognised principle of the parliamentary democracy that the executive is responsible to the popularly elected House of the Parliament where decisions are taken through free discussion and exchange of ideas. In his words,

"It is a method of argument, discussion and decisions, and of accepting that decisions even though one may not agree with it."[11]

Economic and Parliamentary Democracy and Nehru

Jawaharlal Nehru was fully convinced that mere political democracy with its right to vote was not enough. It must lead to the establishment of economic democracy.

Parliamentary government is a democratic conception. Political change by itself is not enough. From political democracy we advance to the concept of economic democracy.[12] As such, Nehru who played a historic role in the fight for the country's freedom was the principal architect of Independent India.[13]

His own training and temperament inevitably led him to chose democratic means and a democratic way of life for the Indian polity. With Nehru at the helm of the state there could be no other path for India to follow, but the path of political democracy. He deliberately opted for parliamentary democracy and a parliamentary form of government in which parliament would be supreme. He gave new content and meaning to parliamentary democracy through a constitution for the country, the cornerstone of which was universal adult franchise. For the first time in India franchise became a matter of birth right for all adults-men and women without any distinction of sex, caste, creed and religion.[14]

His faith in parliamentary democracy flowed from his vision of political democracy. Through his effort, the country as a democratic constitution which enshrined as one of its laudable objectives equality of status and opportunity, social-economic and political justice and dignity of the individual and unity of the nation.

Thus, nationalism, socialism and secularism constituted the main pillars of the edifice of democracy that Nehru sought to build. Whatever Nehru did or thought, democracy was the dominant idea. His socialism was democratic socialism and planning was democratic planning. His concept of planned economic was a kind of mixed economy which comprised both private and public sector.

He firmly laid down democratic means for India and he everstood for democratic process. His contribution to the development of parliamentary democracy and parliamentary institutions have no parallel in history. He lent majestic dignity and authority to parliament. To quote professor Hiren Mukherjee the noted Communist leader.

"Nehru's magnificant role in the fight for our freedom when he was the idol of India's youth, his unique grip on world prospectives which made his realise the link between our fight and the fight of oppressed people in Asia and Africa and elsewhere, his dedication to secularism and democracy and people's well being, which drew him strongly towards socialism, economic planning and world peace all there and more is a matter of record, an open book which his life was."

Nehru, who had stood out of legislatures even after the enactment of the Government of Indian Act, 1935 when the Congress permitted its members to enter of legislatures and even to form ministries in the provinces, made his mark as a parliamentarian of rare gift and ability the moment the entered the central legislature to head the Interim Government in 1946. He took to Parliamentary life like a duck to water and showed an amazing aptitude for parliamentary norms, procedures and conventions.

Jawaharlal Nehru used to speak in the House extempore, and he raraely delivered a written speech except when the importance of the occasion so demanded. He was a great writer but he was equally a great parliamentarian and parliamentary orataor, on all big occasions his speeches were superb performance.

Parliamentary democracy in India was enriched by the high standard and the noble examples Nehru had set.

His Attitude towards Opposition Leaders

The acid test of Nehru's democratic outlook in relation to the functioning of Parliamentary democracy was his attitude to the opposition and the treatment he accorded to the opposition. He sincerely believed that "the parliamentary system of work requires not only a stount opposition, not only forcible expression of opinions and views, but an essential basis of co-operation between the opposition and the government, not in regard to any particular matter but the whole basis of approach is after all a co-operative basis. In so far as we succeeded in doing that, we succeed in laying the foundations of parliamentary work firmly."[16]

The thinness of the opposition did not render its voice ineffective in any way thanks to the democratic values cherished and incalculated by Nehru. At the formation of first Lok Sabha the first Prime Minister advised that although the numerical strength of the opposition was not large, their criticism of Government policies should be given due weight and an attempt should be made to meet their points of criticism and remedial steps taken wherever called for.

He followed democratic norms not only in the functioning of parliament rather in the working of his cabinet also. As a Prime Minister he enjoyed reputation and did not interfare in the functioning of any ministry since all important issues came up before the cabinet decision.

He placed parliamentary democracy in India on a high pedastal, where Parliament was not only the forum of supreme authority, but where freedom of speech and free discussion was real without any rigid party whips or directives. During the formative years of development of parliamentary institutions members of parliament whether belonging to this side or that side had equal freedom of criticising government policies and actions. Many Congress Party members spoke as freely in criticism of Government as it they belong to the opposition parties. At that time there was no organised opposition and it appeared that the responsibility of providing sonews and strength to the opposition rested on the ruling party.

The Congress Party was occupant of the treasury benches and they also partly played the role of opposition in the debates. This was a unique feature of the working of parliamentary democracy under the stewardship of Nehru.

His spirit of extreme tolerance and generosity was evident even during the period of Indian Government. It was not an easy task for Nehru to conduct the House and run the administration in the then prevailing situation.

He was often sharply attacked by the opposition for his Pakistani policies with regard to ill treatment of minorities in

East Pakistan (Now Bangla Desh). On one occasion Pandit Lakshmi Kanta Maitra, a member of the Congress Party expressing his anguishing about a speech of Nehru on the exodus of minorities from East Pakistan under most distressful condition remarked in the Lok Sabha.[17] As I was listening to the Prime Minister I was wondering whether it was the voice of Pandit Jawaharlal Nehru or Liaquat Ali Khan, the Prime Minister of Pakistan. Even such a caustic observation coming from a member of his own party was taken with quite grace by Nehru.

To the opposition, he was even more tolerant and considerable. The plant of parliamentary democracy was carefully nurtured by Nehru so that free discussions and healthy criticism could have full scope without generating any ill feeling. Nehru was a picture of dignity and would not be proved to cast any personal reflections against his opponent even inthe midst of heated or exciting debates.

Once he entered into a sharp[18] passage-at-arms with Dr. Shyama Prasad Mukherjee, Leader of the Jan Sangh Group. Non of the two starwarts was to be outdone by the other in the exchange of retors and repartees. There was a grim silence at the attack and counter attack took a sharper tone. A sense of owe gripped the members on both sides. The speaker G.V. Mavalankar sat motionless in his chair and was not entering with or trying to stop either Dr. Mukherjee or the Prime Minister. The whole House was waiting with bailed breath as to when and how it would end. The fiery exchanges went on for about ten minutes. At last Pandit Govind Malviya from the Congress benches stood up and asked the chair how long the wordy duel would continue. Nehru at once took the hint and calmed down saying", **"I was testing the capacity of Dr. Mukherjee."**

Nehru would never harbour any feeling of bitterness after the debate was over, however, stormy it might be. On one occasion, Sri Atal Bihari Vajpayee, leader of the then Jan

Sangh fired a heavy broadside against the treasury benches and was unsparing in his attack. After the day's proceedings were over in the House, Nehru chanced to meet Mr. Vajpayee at the reception in Rashtrapati Bhawan. The Prime Minister greeted Mr. Vajpayee with a smile on his face saying, **"Aaj to apne Bahut Jabardast Hamala Kiya."**[19]

That was Nehru only a leader of his grace and magnanimity could take such severe attacks in the true parliamentary spirit.

For the success of parliamentary democracy. Nehru was most anxious to build a relationship co-operation between government and the opposition. On every national, international or crucial issue he would invariably take the leaders of the opposition parties and groups into confidence. He was not only tolerant to criticism, but was responsive too, as far as possible.

Being committed to parliamentary form of government. Nehru was ever conscious that the government was wholly answerable to parliament. He used to keep parliament fully informed at all times about all important issues and development concerning the society and the country.

According to Dr. Shankar Dayal Sharma, in a broadcast to the Nation he said, "I have naturally looked to the interest of India for that is my first duty. I have always conceived that duty in terms of the larger good of the world. That is the lession that our master taught us." To Dr. Sharma, Pandit Nehru was a practical idealist. He always talked about India's interests. Once he stated, "I am interested in standing by people who are in great trouble and who have to face tremendous oppression by a powerful government."

Relationship Between the Presiding Officers and Jawaharlal Nehru

Nehru's respect for parliamentary institutions was as deep-rooted as his faith in the democratic process. Parliament symbolised for him the power of the people and he was very zealous of guarding its dignity. In the constitution, composition and functioning of parliament, Nehru has left an indelible mark.

He was ever concious of the fact that sound parliamentary system could be successful and enduring only if speaker was a person of integrity and vision. We were fortunate that he chose G.V. Mavalankar as the first speaker of Lok Sabha.

Speaker Mavalankar, who had the distinction of presiding over India's House of people (Lok Sabha) in the initial years was a great speaker, a born speaker in the words of Pandit Nehru. There was no doubt about his basic uprightness and impartiality. He was precise in his rulings and would insist on correct procedures.

Few, even today, appreciate the key role of Presiding Officer in a parliamentary democracy. The speaker in the all important conventional and ceremonial Head of the House of people (Lok Sabha) and without him the House has no constitutional existance. He is a symbol of impartiality and guardian of the priviledge of the House. He fully understood the significance of the speaker. While speaking in the Lok Sabha on 8th March, 1948, Nehru observed.[20]

"...... The speaker represents the House. He represents the dignity of the House. The freedom of the House and because the House represents the Nation in a particular way, the Speaker becomes the symbol of the nations freedom and liberty. Therefore, it is right that he should be an honoured position, a free position and should occupied always by men of outstanding ability and impartially."

Again speaking in the Lok Sabha on December 18, 1954 on the censure motion against speaker Mavalankar, Nehru made following reference to the office of the Speaker.

"It is not a party matter. It is a matter for this House, for each individual, to consider, regardless of party affiliation. Therefore, let us try to think of it not as a party issue, but as member of this House. It is a serious matter when honour of Parliament is concerned. Speaker, of course, but it affects the first citizen of this country. When we challenge his bonafides we betray before our countrymen and indeed before the world that we are little men and that is the seriousness of the situation.

According to Nehru, the speaker enjoys great power of diseretion and subjective satisfaction in our rules unlike in the other parliament of the world. This became possible because Nehru wanted the Speaker to take the burden of putting our nascent democracy on par with the then developed parliaments such as in United Kingdom in the western countries in as short a time as possible. He had full faitah in the skill and integrity of the Speaker who holds the correct balance between the ruling and the opposition parties to enable the chamber to function efficiently and in the interest of the people whom it represented.

He showed great respect to the House and the Presiding Officers (Speaker and the Chairman) both by his own conduct as the leader of the House. He was fully conscious that speaker, being the spokesman of the House should be as respected as the House itself.

With the speaker's co-operation and help some important inventions of our parliament were built up in his time like:

(a) The introduction of Procedure of Calling Attention notifces.

(b) The establishment of a Committee on Assurance.

(c) The Committee on Public Undertaking etc.

(d) The establishment of Department of Parliamentary Affairs.

Jawaharlal Nehru bowed gracefully to speaker's firm ruling. He built parliamentary traditions of restraint and modernisation, dignity and decorum. He spoke almost always, entirely extempore with a natural fluency, occassionally injecting a dramatic touch. He never tried to hedge or doge and was always ready to admit errors with grace. He was responsive to opposition and many times, during the everflow of his speeches, answered interruptions, permitted by speaker, with case and tolerance. He never showed anger or reluctance to stop answer a member if the speaker wished him to do so.

Nehru was always there in the Lok Sabha as the Leader of the House to carry out his foremost duty of assisting the House and speaker in the conduct of business. He was always co-operative and ready to furnish information or agree debate in difference to the wishes of the speaker.

While Nehru was respectful to the speaker. The Speakers as their part have always been conscious of the fact that Prime Minister has a special position, not only as the leader of the House, but also as the leader of the country.

In a parliamentary democracy, Presiding Officers are not only the guardians of the dignity and priviledges of the House, but by their independence objectively and acumen should promote acceptance by political parties of healthy conventions and traditions which are so necessary for a functioning democracy.

According to him, "The speaker has to abstain from active participation in all the controversial policies. The essence of the matter is that the speaker has to place himself in the position of a judge. The speaker's office can and should be depoliticised by common consent without any further ado and a speaker enable to rise above political temptation and maintain his independence and impartiality.

Leader of the House

Jawaharlal Nehru was a dynamic personality befitting

the high position on the Prime Minister of our great nation. He was a statesman of world calibre. He had established himself throughout the world or an attractive brilliant and a progressive idealist. Infact, he was all human and that made him a very lovable person.[23]

As a leader of the Lok Sabha his refined manners and behavioural dealings amongst the member of parliament endeared himself to one and all in the House. As a true democrat he believe and practised in solving vrious problems through discussions and co-operations and not through confrontations. He liked controversied and welcomed constructive arguments and counter arguments because he saw in then the signs of liveliness.

He was a charismatic mass leader and a champion of the down trodden of the leaning millions in the country. His star quality was that he developed immense affection towards the elected representatives of the people especially those belonging to the opposition parties in parliament.[24]

His outstanding quality was that he was a decent and honourable man and a thorough human per excellence. When he made mistakes, unlike other powerful public figure, he outspokenly admitted his errors and confessed that to 'err is human'. He would even to discuss his own short comings candidly and good humouredly.[25] He rightly obsered,

"Naturally we have to act according to the directions of parliament; which means, according to the wishes of our country and the country men, who are represented in parliament. On this matter there should be no quibbling, no doubt".[26]

He was a strict disciplinarion. He was of the strong view that there would be no, democracy if there was no discipline. His untiring efforts to enfuse discipline in the parliament was found in ample measures. He believed in spick and span in all wake of life. For instance, every day before commencement of the days' proceedings of Lok Sabha, he was seen at 11 a.m. sharp walking into the Lok Sabha chamber to take his allotted seat amogst other. It was really intringuing and at the same time enjoyable to witness from the visitor's gallery every day and before the House commenced its business, how he freely walked down to the opposition benches to great the members with his smiling face wishing them 'good morning' and 'Namaste'. That showed the way how the leader of the Lok Sabha instilled healthy conventions to grow and democratic norms to be maintained in the working of our parliament. As such, he was indeed a true parliamentarian.

REFERENCES

1. Kashyap, Subhash C., *Jawaharlal Nehru and His Constituent*, New Delhi, 1982, p. 41.
2. Patnayak Biju, "Nehru and Parliamentary Democracy" in S.C. Kashyap (Ed.) *Nehru and Parliament*; Lok Sabha Secretariat, New Delhi, 1986, p. 104.
3. "Message of Jawaharlal Nehru to the First Issue" of the *Journal of Parliamentary Information*, Vol. I, No. 1, April, 1955.
4. Nehru Jawaharlal, Addressed at the AICC Indore, 3 January, 1957.
5. Kidwai, Ansari, "*Nehru and working of Democracy*," *op. cit*., p. 81.
6. Nehru Jawaharlal, *Broadcast to the Nation on Independence Day*, 15 August, 1949, Red Fort, New Delhi.
7. Radhakrishna, S., Quoted from R.R. Moraka, "The Father of Parliamentary Democracy in India" in S.C. Kashyap (Ed.), *Nehru and Parliament*, *op. cit*., 1986, p. 58.
8. Nehru Jawaharlal, *Speaking at AICC*, Indore, *op. cit*.
9. Nehru Jawaharlal, *Speaking at Seminar on Parliamentary Democracy*, 25 February, 1956.
10. Nehru Jawaharlal, *Ibid*.
11. Nehru Jawaharlal, *Inaugural Address to the Seminar on Parliamentary Democracy*, 6th December, 1957.

12. Nehru Jawaharlal, *Ibid.*

13. Das, A.N., "Nehru Vision of Parliamentary Democracy" S.C. Kashyap (Ed.), *op. cit.*, p. 69.

14. Srivastava, M.P., *Parliamentary Accountability of Public Enterprises*, Deep & Deep Publications, New Delhi, 1992, p. 20.

15. Shrivastava, M.P., *Problem of Accountability of Public Enterprises in India*, Chugh Publication, New Delhi, 1989, p. 121.

16. *Ibid.*, p. 70.

17. *Ibid.*, p. 72.

18. Lok Sabha Debate, 2nd May, 1963, C. 13404: Lok Sabha Secretariat, New Delhi.

19. *Ibid.*, p. 73, Lok Sabha Debate, 1959, p. 169.

20. Shakdhar, S.L., "Nehru and Presiding Officer" in *Nehru and Parliament* (Ed.), S.L. Shekdhar, Lok Sabha Secretariat, p. 161.

21. *Ibid.*

22. *Ibid.*, p. 169.

23. Gangadeb, P., As the leader of the Lok Sabha in S.C. Kashyap (Ed.) *Nehru and Parliament*, *op. cit.*, p. 191.

24. *Ibid.*

25. *Ibid.*

26. *Lok Sabha Debate*, IXth session, 1959, Vol. XXV, p. 1686, Lok Sabha Secretariat, New Delhi.

7

Relevance of Socio-Economic Ideas of Nehru in New Economic Reform and Globalisation

Just after Independence of India on 15th August, 1947, Indian economy, under the premiership of Jawaharlal Nehru, was built through planning in the lines of Soviet Russia. Due to global significance of the socio-economic ideas of Jawaharlal Nehru economic development was adopted as national motto. Five Year Planning has been continuing since 1st April, 1951. Uptill now we have completed nine five year plans and five annual plans in total.

Nehru's Ideas and Globalisation

His ideas are still very useful in terms of globalisation, liberalisation and economic reform. In the context of globalisation this chapter makes an attempt to examine the role of the socio-economic ideas of Nehru.

Globalisation implies a regime of competitive markets with no entry or exist barrier. Globalisation is the professed goal of the on going economic reforms in India.[1] Globalisation means increasing integration of developing countries into the global economy. It is achieved through liberalisation of trade and capital market, increasing internationalisation of corporate production and technological change that is rapidly dismantling barriers to the international trade ability of goods and services and the mobility of capital.

According to Nehru we live in increasingly interdependent world and perhaps some day we will live in a "world without borders" to borrow from the title of a provocative book of 1970. For developing countries, dependence on rich nations is and has been always a stark fact of economic life. It is the principal reason for their heightened interest in promoting greater individual and collective self-reliance. At the same time, the developed world, which once prided itself on its apparent economic self-sufficiency, has come to realise that in an age of increasingly scarce natural and mineral resources, global environment threats, accelerated international illegation migration, and burgeoning world trase, it too is becoming ever more economically dependent on the developing world.

According to United Nations Trade & Development Report, 1997 (New York) "Since the 1960s, remarkable globalisation of the world economic has taken place.

The economic reform programmes with globalisation, marketisation and privatisation, have been launched since 1991. The stress of the programme has been to bring about a real market economy and seek an increased role of India economy with global economic system. The core components of reform programme are:

1. Industrial policy reforms.
2. Trade policy and exchange control reform.
3. Financial sector reforms.
4. Public enterprises reforms.

5. Fiscal reforms and
6. Increased direct foreign investment.

The current economic reform being carried out by Government of India has been described as basically a shift from central planning to a market driven economic system. India has the potential of becoming one of the largest common markets in the world and there can be greater division of labour, freedom of mobility of capital and labour as well as of greater inter-regional trade. The implementation of a policy of liberalisation on various fronts was not only a bold step but a challenging one.

The economic reforms since 1991 have resulted in some fundamental changes in trade, financial, fiscal, industrial and foreign investment policies. Several stabilisation measures have been introduced to tackle the problem of liquidity.

The development landscape is being transformed, presenting policy-makers with new challenges at the global and local level. This chapter charts the way forward by analysing the contours of the new landscape and distilling lessons from the past. It examines the unfolding dynamic at the supernational and subnational levels.

Fifty Five years of development experience have yielded four critical lessons. First, macroeconomic stability is an essential pre-requisite for achieving the growth needed for development. Second, growth does not trickle down, development must address human needs directly. Third, no one policy will trigger development. Fourth, institutions matter, sustained development should be rooted in process that are socially inclusive and responsive to changing circumstances. To reducing poverty, these challenges include issues of food security water scarcity, aging populations, cultural loss and environmental degradation. These challenges must be confronted even as many forces reshape the development terrain; innovations in technology. The spread of knowledge, the growth of population and its concentration in cities, the financial integration of the world, and rising demands for political and human rights. If they are managed well, these forces could revolutionize the prospects for development and human welfare.

Globalisation of production or location of multi plants of a single firm in countries found suitable, is rooted in the development of capitalism.[2] While globalisation in trade and commerce is nothing new, globalisation aimed at establishment of a new international economic order in capitalist globalisation of production is an event of the recent past.

Like Nehru we may like his assumption for the operation of firms within the capitalist production system:

1. for any firm, profit maximisation or its proxy, e.g. sales maximisation, subject to minimum profit constraint;
2. for all firms taken together, non-redundancy of labour even in the context of technological improvement.

Location of Plants

Location of plant by a firm, operating as or trying to be a transitional is conditional upon the existence of a labour force ready to sell labour-power at any positive acceptable price considered minimum to the owner of non-labour resources.

Cheap Labour

The 'cheap labour' arguments of Nehru can also stand on the following arguments among others:

(i) Unlimited supply of labourers, mostly unskilled.

(ii) Positive and sizeable unemployment, maintained blow the level that may bring about political risk, but the role that is necessary for the multi plant firms to expect downward pressure on the wage rate.

(iii) Keeping an informal sector for absorption of labourers in the formal sector who face exist and for the job seekers in general.

(iv) Socio-political apathy toward the unemployed often called unemployable.

(v) Government centred society or social group.

(vi) Non-existence of labour legislation.

(vii) Weak labour legislation.

(viii) Weak Trade Unions or Trade Union working at Cross purposes.

Laissez Fair Idea and Economic Reforms

His idea of laissez fair policy is directly related to present economic reform and globalisation policy. In 1990s all the countries is the Third World were found entangled in the web of capitalism supervised by the Development Market Economic (DMEs), particularly following the end of cold war. Given the division of the countries in terms of resources and technology, the countries constituting the third world are compelled to accept the conditionalities imposed by the Bretton Woods twins, World Bank & I.M.F. as reflected in structural Adjustment Programme (SAP).[3] The ready reflection, for example for India is New Economic Policy 1991, declared by the Government of India by Dr. Manmohan Singh. This compulsion is comonflaged as choice in the name a development strategy which may be called open door for industrialization.

His ISI Strategy & Liberalisation

The ISI strategy was adopted in India by Jawaharlal Nehru which was explicitly incorporated in India's second five year plan (1956-61) and was expected to pave the way for export promotion efforts over a sufficient broad based. Due to Nehru in the planned gradual transformation of the economy, the state was supposed to play the key role.[4] In a mixed capitalist economic structure which we proposed the establish the role of the state was supposed to be led by public sector enterprises where these public sector enterprises were assigned the task of producing capital goods and thereby commanding the economy.

The ISI strategy relied on a probable shift from pre-independence export led exploitation for building up the base for internal production and hence expansion of home market. The strategy also relied on protecting indigenous technology and infant industries with a view to making them strong enough to ultimately compete in the international market. This strategy of Nehru was adopted for it political fasibility during the 1950s and early 1980s. But in certain quarters, the strategy was considered autarky.

Table I

Growth Rate of Industrial Production and Import Availability Ratio

(Per cent 1951-56) (Base year 1956)

Industries	*Growth*		*Rates*	*Imports*	
	1951-55	*1965-66*	*1960-65*	*1959-60*	*1965-66*
Total	5.7	7.2	9.6	18.1	14.1
A. Use Based Classification					
a. Basic Goods	4.7	12.0	10.4	34.1	22.5
b. Intermediate	7.8	6.4	6.9	21.3	10.9
c. Capital	9.8	13.1	19.6	44.0	36.4
d. Consumer	4.8	4.4	4.9	5.7	4.9
B. Input Based Classification					
a. Agro-based	4.0	3.8	4.0	4.7	2.7
b. Metal based	7.5	14.1	18.2	39.3	31.6
c. Clenical-based	8.5	12.2	9.0	35.3	21.9

Source: S.L. Shetty, *Structural Retrogression in the Indian Economy Since Mid Sixties. (Economic Political Weekly)* Vol. XIIJ (Annual No.) Feb. 1998, p. 186 & I.J. Ahluwalia, *Industrial Growth in India Stagnation since Mid Sixties OPU*, 1985, p. 9, 21, 120 (For import availability ratio).

Table II
Import by Exhaustive Components as Percentage of Total Imports (1951-64)

Plan	*Period*	*Capital Goods*	*Consumer Goods*	*Maintenance Goods*
First	1951-56	21.38	24.95	48.83
Second	1956-61	29.24	17.74	47.39
Third	1961-64	34.87	16.51	43.79

Source: NCAER (1967), *Maintenance Import*, New Delhi, p. 2.

Table I shows reduced import availability ratio in 1965-66 relative to those in 1959-60 which is a state of generally high and accelerating industrial growth. Only the basic goods under the use based classification and chemical based goods under input based classification show some deceleration.

Table II shows that it was relatively easy to reduce imports of consumer goods as percentage of total imports, relative to that of reducing imports of capital goods and maintenance imports. The inability to reduce the share of capital goods and maintenance goods is to be judged in the context of an initial weak supply of capital goods relative to requirement of capital goods needed for industrialisation as prescribed by Mahalnobis.

Table III shows the import availability ratio for foodgrains, fertilizers and tractors, on each from consumer goods, capital goods and maintenance imports.

Table IV shows our trade balance its ratio with GDP and the position of foreign exchange reserves.

In sum, while growth performance on the industrial front was not bad, we did not perform well in terms of trade balance and were faced external liquidity crisis at the period of Jawaharlal Nehru.

Table III
Import Availability Ratio (%) 1955-56

Year	*Food grain*	*Fertilizers*	*Tractors*
1955-56	2.2	40.64	–
1960-61	4.6	73.64	–
1961-62	4.8	61.14	77.30
1962-63	6.1	53.34	64.91
1963-64	8.0	46.85	54.19
1964-65	8.8	44.87	34.95
1965-66	14.1	54.56	25.82
Third Plan (1961-66)	8.31	51.89	46.16

Source: *Govt. of India, Economic Survey*, 1983-84, pp.94-95 (for food and fertilizers), NCAER, 1980. Implication of Tractionasation for farm Employment, Productivity and Income Vol. I, p.53 (for tractors).

Table IV
Trade Balance & Foreign Exchange Reserve (Rs. Crore) 1951-66

Year	*Trade Balance*	*Trade Balance GDP Ratio*	*Foreign Exchange Changes Reserve*
1951-52	– 174	– 1.75	864
1955-56	– 165	– 1.61	902
1960-61	– 480	– 2.96	304
1961-62	– 430	– 2.50	297
1962-63	– 446	– 2.41	295
1963-64	– 430	– 2.02	306
1964-65	– 533	– 2.15	250
1965-66	– 599	– 2.29	298

Source: Ibid.

We find that the economy took a U-turn during post-1966 period which incidently coincided with a number of external shocks, including the significant devaluation in June 1966. The pre-1966 quantitative controls led to the protection domestic industries irrespective of cost structure leading to inefficient import substitution. The post-1966 emergence of excess capacity in capital goods sector was supposed to be tackled by vent for surplus. Thus, the shift from ISI to EOI may be interpreted as a shift from dependence on home market to independence on world market. This was a period particularly seventies and eighties, when the potential exporters got high export assistance from Government of India particularly industries producies engineering and chemical goods. It led to a slight size in exports of engineering goods as a percentage of India's total exports, but could not ensure increasing command on global front. By the mid sixties India came to assure less than one per cent of world exports and stagnated at half of one per cent from mid seventies. All these had their effects on trade balance and foreign exchange reserves.

NEP 1991 & NEHRU

The New Economic Policy introduced since 1991 made it clear that India can grow faster as part of the world economy and not in isolation. Our trade policy must therefore, create an environment that will provide story impetus to exports and render export activity profitable. The package of trade policy reforms announced in July, 1991 aimed at access to high technology and world markets.

The economic reform, thus, aimed at strengthening export incentives eliminating a substantial volume of import licensing and optimal import compression in view of the balance of payment situation. The New Policy aims at reducing the interference of government if not totally abolish it, in matters related to import of technology by Indian firms particularly in high technology and high investment priority industries.

The New Industries-cum-trade policies thus, reveal an

"input liberalizing-cum-export promoting" or what we call an ODI strategy.

Profit Motive in Present Context

In an acquisitive society based on profit-motive, appeared Jawaharlal Nehru out of date in the new world that is growing up, it does not mean that there should no incentives. Though, incentives may not be confirmed to financial benefits, may always be necessary. Jawaharlal Nehru was against profit-motive. He revealed that in the context of world today, such a motive is becoming increasing not only wrong from the economic point of view, but a vulgar thing from any sensitive point of view changes are bound to repeat.

Nehru was against free economy. To him, laissez faire vaariety of economic policy brought the law of jungle which was called by Carlyle as 'Pig-philosophy'. The theory of individual freedom failed at the period of Nehru but it has again become effective and useful at the present stage. He observed that liberty of the individual in the laissez faire economy was a mere myth in itself.

His democracy under laissez-faire is very significant even today as he maintained that democracy under laissez-faire was only a political democracy not economic democracy. Without equality democracy and liberty have no meaning at all.

But, now all centralisation is a sight encroachment in the freedom of the individual. To him, the real problem of India economy was maintaining balance between the two. He argued that the political right of individual be safeguarded by the constitution of the state. He believed in a policy of flexibility in term of economic function of the state.

His Capitalism in Present Context

He maintained that capitalism is still very significant as its kinds exists in all countries of the world. Despite great opposition he recognised the contribution of capitalism.

He rightly observed that industrial capitalism in older age was acclaimed as the saviour of human being becauise of modernising production. In the global field capitalism breeds conflicts and colonialism, as it must have global markets to dump surplus goods. Capitalism has outlived its usefulness in the context of present social aspiration and economic condition. But according to him, capitalism is not only system in the world which had to face decadence. Economic systems springs from the dynamics of life and are envolved to meet the prevailing needs and requirements of a community.

Nehru's Ideas of Poverty in Economic Reform

India is a poor country, our development efforts during the last fifty five years have always aimed at reduction in the incidence and severity of poverty across masses scattered over different regions and states. It is well known result that the decline in the incidence of rural poverty is very closely associated with the growth in the agricultural sector particularly in the agricultural productivity over the years. The record of poverty alleviation varied significantly across states of India and across rural and urban areas. Education and health care are two important elements in the process of elevation of one's well being and capability in the long run.

Unless the programmes for rural infrastructure development like extension of irrigation facilities and land distribution are accompanied by carefully thought out schemes for taxing the beneficiaries of rural investment and development and investigating the surplus so acquired for the betterment of the true have nots in the rural economy, the macro programmes like Jawahar Rojgar Yojna (JRY) and/or land distribution, even if meticulously implemented will not be able to eradicate poverty among the bottom layers of income distribution.

The principle of decentralised decision-making has been accepted in the Tenth Five Year Plan to strengthen and effective implementation of rural poverty alleviation programmes in our country. Efforts should be taken to devise institutional mechanisms to pre-empt differentiation of benefits among the rural poor as a consequence of adoption and implementation of poverty alleviation programme in general.

L.P.G. and Its Impact and Nehru

The Indian economic policy had a complete turn around in 1991, when we had chosen to shift from the phase of the command economy to the phase of the economic liberalisation privatisation and globalisation (LPG). It is however, worth noting that basic motivation of initiating these reforms has been to make our industries efficient and globally competitive and not to make the poor people of the country better off in the immediate run. Some economists feared that the incidence of poverty will shoot up following relaxation of state controls and reliance on marked based incentives to drive the forces of growth to the ulter neglect of distributive support policies.

Except for the first year after introduction of reforms, when the rate of inflation was not still diminished, there has not been any remarkable increase in the incidence of rural poverty, and urban poverty in fact fluctuated, first rising since 1991, and then falling. There is no conclusive evidence of immunization of the living condition of the poor because of introduction of reform package, as the economy experienced good mansoon in successive years. There is no immediate prospect of large scale reforms in our agricultural sector to step up its growth rate, and hence poverty reduction through the process of liberalisation and globalisation seems unliked. But there are also direct impacts that are possible with globalisation and liberalisation likely to affect growth and profitability of indigenous industrial enterprises, the renewed dependence on the agrarian economy for further employment creation may have the effects of reducing the rural wage rates in the medium run, which can be circumvented only by raising the productivity of the agricultural sector through diversification of product base.

Poverty Alleviation

Given the strong inverse association between the incidence of rural poverty and the rural wage rates, the moot question is whether the government should go for full scale globalisation of agriculture and allied busines activities in the immediate run or not to achieve these objectives.

Moreover, poverty reductions in rural and urban areas in the ultimate analysis would require massive investment in physical and human infrastructure so as to accelerate the tempo of growth which will ultimately moderate poverty and this is related to the ultimate sharing of this burden of high investment between the private and the state sector.

Thus, a new dimension of the relationship between the state and the market in an era of economic liberalisation should constitute the political economy of poverty alleviation and public action in India.

In a nut shell, this is the core of the fundamental challenge that faces the nation at the stroke of the golden jubilee of its political independence. Poverty in Indian economy is a historical problem and we have a long way to go to eradicate it in all its dimensions in the new century. The immediate task seems to be to devise proper institutional machanism to ensure growth with distribution without wastage among income groups and across regions and make our industrial structure employment intensive, yet efficient and globally competitive. A paradigm shift in our policy formulation seems to be an urgent necessity.

According to World Development Report 2003

The concentration of poverty in a particular group suggests that decision makers are not receptive to signals, especially from the fringes, and national potential is being wasted. "Governments need to move to nondiscriminatory policies and help those in extreme poverty".

The views of Nehru are globally acknowledged. To quote World Development Report 2003 (p. 182). Accelerated growth in productivity and income can eliminate poverty and enhance prosperity is developing countries. This growth needs to be achieved at the same time critical ecosystem services are improved and social fabric that underpins development is strengthened.

Concern stems from evidence that getting the world on a sustainable path is problematic:

— In many developing countries, productivity is low, grwoth is stagnant, and unemployment is high.

— The number of people living on less than $1 a day (1-2 bullion) is dropping but it is still a challenge, and more people are living on frgile lands.

— Income inequality is rising. Average income in the wealthiest-20 countries is 37 times that in the poorest 20 countries-Twice the ratio in 1970.

— Many of the poorest countries are wracked by civil conflict, with animosities deep and prolonged.

— Stress on the environment is increasing. Fisheries are being over exploited, soil degraded, coral reefs destroyed, tropical forests lost, air and water polluted.

— The financial transfers to address these issues are far from adquate, even though the resources are available.

The incidence of poverty may have declined but its

severity as well as the number of the poor people and the tasks of alleviating their poverty in multiple dimensions in a changed environment of globalisation and liberalisation remain a serious one. This is a challenge to our policy makers to development strategies and solution to the multitudes of problems associated with poverty alleviation and growth for better life in the new century.

Jawahar Rojgar Yojana

Keeping in view the ideas of Nehru, theoretically there is little open unemployment in villages but poverty is open. People are all the time moving for jobs in informal sectors but this only holds employment and poverty together. On the other hand, there are people who have no work but they are not poor. This is due to the wide disparity in ownership of assets. The landed middle class only shares the benefits of both worlds depriving the poor of what might have gone to them and allowing the rich to keep on. Poverty, thus, lingers as a systematic feature, making the wage employment approach only a weak palliative. The failure of Jawahar Rojgar Yojna or even self-employment scheme of the integrated rural projects are due to the autagonism in the system itself. As regression in consumption is much lower than that in income, even one day employment is a week could raise up consumption over a poverty line. But a lot of efforts are needed to raise up incomes and assets unless there is a structural change.

Land Reform

There has been another policy flow of approaching village poverty as a wage problem because the surplus labour can be easily dispensed with by transfer to other wage sectors. Such employments are supposed to be springing up under the trickle down effects of urban growth. Infact the socalled redundant zero productive labour would hamper agriculture if transferred, besides the fact that such transfers would be costly and casual. What was needed in a massive poverty eradication scheme was the growth of land substitutory factors like irrigation and growth of complementary capital within the villages accompanied with the policy input of land reform.

The existence of long term constancy of various ratios like labour employed and capital output on land bears out the view. Land reform, as important policy variable is important to the problem of poverty as it provides a ground for changing production relations and the implicat incentives and risk taking capacity of the cultivators. If poverty has lingered it is only due to the failure to land reforms which is missing perspective in the theory of economic development.

Low utilisation rate of land resources under such unequal system where most of the people are landless or nearly landless are the main causes to linger poverty like the views of Nehru. The freerer flow of imports under the reforms would further make demand for domestic labour fall. The infrastructures facilities to villages by the state are found to be biased in favour of richer farmers.

It is revealed that the New Economic Policy has not even diluted the problem of educated unemployment and thus, the structural adjustment programme is not an employment intensive one in India. In short the New Economic Reform[5] in India has led to the following conclusions:

1. The liberalisation programmes have promoted the attention of more capital intensive industries, resulted into decentralised production and relatively high direct transition cost of labour in organised sectors. Thus, the major share of new employment is likely to take place in the former sector.
2. The retrenchment of work force under existing policy is inevitable under the banner of voluntary retirement in public sector units and closing down of sick units in private sector will result into high unemployment

and high degree of incidence of poverty and therefore, is an anti-welfare policy from social point of view.

3. The liberalised policy has resulted into flexibilisation of labour i.e. on rise in employment of temporary, casual and contract labourers due to the labour saving technology. The casualisation of labour will lead to deterioration in workign condition, economic status as well as to the health condition of these labourers.

4. The decentralised production strategy encourages the capitalistic mode of production and in such a mode of production the labourer will not be benefitted from optimum production. As a result, the variation in income distribution will get widened and thus, will encourage the concentration of economic power.

The worst affected sector in employment generation under the New Economic Policy/Reform is the agricultural sector, where the GDP growth rate for five decades recorded only 2.45 percent and is very low and at the time the dependency rate of same is more than 70 per cent.[6]

As such, in order to boost agricultural sector large volume of public investment especially in areas of irrigation and pro-technology are required the only GDP growth rate and rural employment can be generated through secondary and tertiary sectors under the New Economic Reform, more emphasis on diversification of agriculture is given. However, these developments are only limited to horticulture, floriculture, and aquaculture.

No doubt, these developments will improve the returns per unit area, generate more employment in secondary and tertiary sector and raise foreign exchange earnings. However, post-harvest technological facilities are limited in India. The assurance of post-harvest handing technology and adequate credit and marketing facilities are the pre-conditions in order to reap maximum advantage from these activities.

The entry of foreign collaborated firms in fishing will adversally affect the employment in this subsector. The other subsectors of primary sector viz. forestory, bee keeping and mushroom farming etc. are also required to be encouraged, so that, with less capital investment more employment generation can be promised in rural sector.

Similarly enterpreneureal skills should be promoted for encouraging more self employment. All these developments will have an effect on the employment in the service sector for instance, design, planning, distribution of finance, consultancy, counselling etc. similarly, social services sectors also should be given due importance through which employment generation is possible in the short run as well as promise a better tomorrow. The activities of multinational corporation are limited more in the urban and semi-urban areas and their activities should be expanded to economically backward regions of the country too, so that the benefits of liberalisation can help the transformation of these areas considerably[3].

No doubt, India is a labour-surplus nation. The operation of the market economy will not give due justice to the various sectors of the society as well as to the various sections of the people. Of course, the state has a positive role to solve the multivaried economic and social probloem in an economy like ours. This conclusion directly relates to the conclusions of Jawaharlal Nehru.

Like many developing countries, India has slowly but surely moved towards a more market oriented, market friendly economy as a result of liberal economic policies with less and less government, privatization public enterprises, lower taxes deregulation of the labour market and free and open foreign trade.

The scoio-economic ideas of Jawaharlal Nehru can easily be assessed in terms of globalisation, liberalization, privatization and economic reform. His ideas were mainly consisted of:

A. Laissez-faire Policy

(i.e. theoretical freedom of each individual to work:)

(i) unlimited acquisitiveness or profit motive;

(ii) free enterprises in a state of perfect competition;

(iii) monopoly of property in the material means of production;

(iv) relationship between state and individual;

(v) free and controlled efforts of Nehru;

(vi) democracy under Laissez-faire;

(vii) joint sector and mixed economy;

(viii) paradox of poor remains poorer and rich remain richer;

(ix) position of poor consumer;

(x) position of poor productor or investor;

(xi) evil effects of monopolies;

(xii) democracy and capitalism;

(xiii) relevance of capitalism;

B. Agriculture and Land Reform/Rural Development

(a) zamindar

(b) division of land sub-division and fragmentation of holdings.

(c) land reforms - objectives, evils and measures.

(d) infrastructural development.

(e) agricultural credit and inputs.

(f) co-operative farming.

(g) panchayati raj, rural development.

C. Industry

(a) industrialisation - industrial revolution.

(b) large scale industries.

(c) cottage and small scale industries.

(d) khadi industries.

(e) community service.

(f) co-operation.

D. Capital Farmation

E. Population Problems and Policy

F. Public Finance

(a) taxation.

(b) public expenditure.

(c) public debt.

(d) deficit budget.

(e) foreign exchange reserves.

G. Stages of Economic Growth

H. Trade and Commerce

(a) balance of payment.

(b) terms of trade.

(c) direction of trade.

(d) trade policy.

(e) foreign exchange.

(f) financial sector.

(g) private and public investment.

(h) multinational corporation.

I. Economic Order

Scientific and technological progress, their role, problems etc.

J. Socialism

(a) socialism and growth.

(b) socialistic pattern of society.

(c) problem of inequality and injustice, poverty etc.

(d) problem of unemployment and rural backwardness.

(e) regional embalance.

K. Public Sector - Role, Objectives, Working Problems etc.

L. Planning Needs, Objectives, Forms, Evils, Merits and Demerits, Relevance etc.

M. Education, Health etc.

Structure Adjustment and Nehru

Several Third World nations including India are passing through a rather difficult and painful transition, referred to as adjustment due to above noted changes. As a vast majority of people live in rural areas an important area of concern in this adjustment process is obviously the economic conditions of the rural population in particular, that of the large number consists of the female agricultural workers. According to World Development Report. The World Bank (1995) on Workers in an Integrated World the continued economic liberalization and globalization policies in India and in other countries would result is greater demand for unskilled labour and inequalities may be minimised. The real challenges in India are as stresses the World Bank to raise rural incomes to reduce poverty.

The package of economic reforms constitutes a sharp turn around in policy thinking compared the 'licence permit raj' built up during 1960's and 1970's.

Thus to some extent the ideas and formulas were reverted under L.P.G. (Liberalisation, Privatization and Globalization) economic reform.

Deregulation for Small Scale Sector

Under the present process of economic reforms the stranglehold of regulation appears to have only increased in respect of the entire class of small producers. It does not attempt to breakdown the innumerable hurdles faced by small industries, small entrepreneurs, small farmers who compromise the bulk of the population. One can without doubt, say that many of the controls that affect small producers are within the jurisdiction of state governments. Yet, it would be equally true to say that[8] the liberalisation process has totally neglected their interests of small producers. In fact, the financial sector reforms are directly antithetical to their interests and have positively encouraged economic concentration.[9]

The real problem in the present approach is the total neglect of the bulk of Indian producers and Indian consumers.[10] It is only elite who are the beneficiaries of the ongoing policies.

In this context three basic points are relevant:

(a) Before the average Indian has been properly educated and imparted skills, he is forced to face unfettered competition from economically stronger competitors. In fact, the competition is unfair between unequal.

(b) For private rent seeking India is making all

infrastructure as well as key product needlessly expensive; and it is thereby raising industrial and farming costs to uncompetitive and unsustainable levels in the future.

(c) In the guise of seeking the latest technology India is destroying indigenous research and development capability.

Nationalisation

As regards, views of India National Congress on Nationalisation, the views of Nehru were very useful. Ever since the Nagpur Congress of 1891, the Congress at each annual session of its sitting drew attention to the economic maladies of the Nation and suggested means to overcome them. Among those means, nationalisation almost always had been allotted some role to play. Ideas were gradually developing and what was nubulous and vague began to take a clear shape only since the late twenties of the century. Moreover, instead of defining a general attitude towards the development of entire economy is such, attention seems to have been paid to individual burning issues, like famine and protection to their or that industry.

It was at Karanchi Congress for the first time that the Congress attempted define its attitude towards the future course of the developmetn of the economy of the country.

In 1937[11], when Congress came to power in several provinces as a sequal to partial acceptance to the Government of India Act, 1935[12], the then President of the Congress Subhash Chandra Bose gathered together a conference of Ministers of Industries of the various provinces to consider the question of economic development in all its bearing. The conference emphasised the need for industrialisation and recommended for drawing up a comprehensive national plan for this.

National Planning Committee

As a result of this recommendation 8th direction of the Act, Indian Congress Working Committee the National Planning Committee under the chairmanship of Pandit Jawaharlal Nehru came into being. The recommendations of this committee constitute a land mark because they contain the essentials of the economic objectives of the Congress.

The Committee classified industries into defence, key and public utility and recommended that these be owned and operated by the state. Industries recommended for being state owned by the committee were the following:

(a) power, hydro and thermal generator.

(b) fuel, coal and fuel-wood, mineral oil, power, alcohal and national gas.

(c) metal, ferrous and important non-ferrous including winning of one of them.

(d) industries for the making for machine tools.

(e) industries for the making of machinery and machine parts.

(f) heavy engineering industries for the building of ships, locomotives, wagons, automobiles, air crafts and the like.

(g) instruments and apparatus commercial, industrial and scientific standards.

(h) chemicals, heavy chemicals, fine chemicals including only (some-vital) fertilizers and refractories.

The list of the public utility included[13]:

(a) distribution of electricity gas and other forms of energy.

(b) public transport and communication services.

(c) water supply and

(d) sanitation.

Those were the days when all the left luminaries of the erstwhile Socialist Party like Narendra Deo, Jai Prakash Narain, Sri Ashok Mehta etc. were important persons inside the Congress. They understood the problems and did much to convert the Congress to their point of view.

In October, 1938 the National Planning Committee under the chairman Nehru was set up to keep in readiness plans to meliorate suffering and improve the conditions of fanished millions of India who had been groaning under British yoke and make them enjoy the sunshine of freedom.

Position of Private Enterprises

Private enterprise was not ruled out but would have to be strictly controlled and co-ordinated to the general plan. He rejected the Gandhian view point that machinery was evil in itself and he resigned from the Executive Committee of the All India Spinners Association.

Objectives of Socio-economic Ideas of Nehru

The main socio-economic ideas of Jawaharlal Nehru was to make India economically strong, stable and self-sufficient so that economic and political freedom might be meaningful. His all these ideas and thinkings should be viewed in the context of the Indian social and economic setting. His ideas of mixed economy, planning, socialism, industrialisation, agriculture and co-operation etc. were all directed towards a strong foundation of the shattered economy of India.

India suffered from inefficiency of production, inequality of distribution and instability of economic life at the time of economic planning. The result of his socio-economic ideas during the period ranging from 1950-51 to 1965-66 was an overall strengthening of the Indian economy and its heading towards desired goals. The national income at constant (1948-49) prices went up from Rs. 8850 crores in 1950-51 to Rs. 14930 crores in 1964-65 and the per capital income from Rs.247.5 to Rs. 314.4 (both at constant prices). During 15 years index number of agricultural production of all commodities (1949-50 = 100) rose from 95.6 to 157.6 and index of industrial production (1956 = 100) increased from 73.5 in 1951 to 174.8 in 1964-65.[14]

Similar progress was registered in the power generation, construction of roads and development of other means of transport and communication. In addition to there material achievements, consequent upon his economic ideas and their execution, there was a change in the motivation pattern and ways of thinking and doing of the Indian people. In fact, the Indian economy changed from a position of stagnation and tradition to dynamism and modernity.

Present Economic Planning and Nehru

His ideas on economic planning included in its orbit addoption of democratic socialism, development of basic and heavy industries, beginning of land reform and co-operatives for agricultural re-organisation. In most of these directions a satisfactory rate of progress was achieved in spite of several shortfalls, pitfalls and unfavourable climate for development. It went a long way in building up the modern India and prevented her from stepped towards military rule like other developing nations of Asia and Africa. To quote Mr. S. Kesava Iyenger. "The democratic planning in India with about 450 million population is undoubtedly the most significant experiment without any per cent of parallel any where in the world."[15]

The deviction for the ideas and thinking from Nehru in present global perspective has also resulted inefficiency of production, inequality of distribution and instability of economic and political instability.

An elaborate study of Nehru's economic policies lead us to the conclusion that Nehru believed that for full reaslisation of political and social freedom it was essential to have economic freedom for 'there could be no real freedom without economic freedom. To call a starving man free is but to mock him".[16] Full fledge political freedom means progressively what might broadly be called economic freedom. According to him.

"To give an opportunity to large number of people to profit by democratic method and to have more or less equal chances to progress".[17] A political vote has its own value but it is useless "if it is decompanied by hunger and starvation".[18] Nehru defined economic freedom thus. Firm of all, that means working for a certain measure of well being for all, call it welfare state. Secondly, at means working for a certain measure of equality of opportunity in the economic sphere.[19]

Economic Freedom

His concept of economic freedom included an economic structure based on:

(a) economic equality

(b) on the well being of the masses, and

(c) on co-operative spirit.

His ideal of an egalitarian society was "a co-operative ideal based on social justice and economic equality."[20] In 1995, while speaking at Trichur Nehru announced, "I also want a classless society in India and the world. I do not want any privileged class. I do not want a great deal of inequality among people."[21]

He was very critical of prevailing economic inequality in society maldistribution of wealth and the control of government by the privileged class. He condemned a society where some people live in luxury without doing any work, whilst others work from morning to might with no rest or leisure and yet have not got the barest necessities of life.[22] Such a society is complete negation of freedomand can never be called a just society. At Jhansi 1928 while making a speech he stated.

Our economic programme must aim at the removal of all economic inequality and an equaitable distribution of wealth".[23]

To him the main aim of free society is to reduce the gap between the favoured fewed and unfavoured millions.[24]

Economic freedom as such, included a socio-economic structure which would ensure minimum opportunities for the physical and social well-being of its members, which would eliminate exploitation and disparities and thus provide for the self development of the individual. In other words, economic freedom was the central point round which, the whole socio-economic and political ideas and convictions of Jawaharlal Nehru were woven. He was fully convinced that economic freedom was the basis for all other freedoms. His socialism was not pure socialism.

Building up a New Modernised India

After Independence his efforts were concentrted on building up a new modernised India on socialistic pattern of society through democratic process. His own experience of the miseries of the Indian peasants, workers and masses confirmed his faith in a goal of socialistic society. He tried his level best to put Indian economy on the path of planned economic development by constituting Planning Commission in 1950 and National Development Council while prepared blue print of three five year plans under his dynamic leadership and guidance. He believed that socialism was not only a system of socio-economic organisations but something deeper which involves a way of thinking and living. Socialism is based on the growth of material resources as well as social justice and co-operative method of working.

Unflicting Faith in Co-operation

Jawaharlal Nehru had an unflincting faith in co-operation because to him co-operation helps actively in effectuation of democratic socialism and peaceful economic change. According to him, "I have no doubt theoretically in co-operation. Co-operation working is good in every single department of human activities. It is a better way of life. Like a true and veteran co-operator he stood for a principle of voluntarism and self-help through mutual help".[25]

Summing up

India is an under-developed country with limited capital and skills both in private and public sectors. A steady increase in production is the prime requisite, if the basic goal of a higher standard of living for the masses is to be achieved, both public and private capital have important role to play, to use public funds for nationalisation of existing industry is both short, sighted and foolhardy.[26] We must also think beyond the immediate wants of the present and utilise our resources with foresight.[27]

As regards welfare state, while placing economic and social planning in the concurrent list the constitution vested power in the union to ensure co-ordinated development in essential fields of activities while presenting the initiative and the authority of the states in spheres allotted to them. Planning was sumerised to be an instrument of using in a democratic socialistic secular, republic order or society in the country.[28]

Jawaharlal Nehru had a pragmatic practical intellectual and idealist approach to lead the country in the right direction. He wished that people should understand his approach in the light of long term objectives.[29]

In India, according to Nehru planning and the active intervention by the state in economy were indispensable. The key industries must inevitably, be controlled very closely by the state. The industrial power is our prime need. Without this we can achieve little.

His ideas and contribution regarding agriculture development are very crucial even today at the age of globalisation. To him, agriculture was one of the most significant discoveries of mankind. On 17th November, 1952, while delivering lecture on the silver jubilee celebration of Central Board of Irrigation and Power, New Delhi he rightly stated. "The biggest development in the history of humanity was, I suppose the discovery of agriculture".[30] On 15th December, 1955 he announced in the Parliament "If our agricultural foundation is not strong the industry we seek to build will not have a strong basis either."[31] Apart from that the situation in the country today is such that our fore front cracks up, every thing else will crack up too. Therefore, we dare not weaken our food front. If our agriculture becomes strongly entremented even it will be relatively easy for us to progress more rapidly on the industrial front.[32]

Jawaharlal Nehru evinced on immense interest in peasants and agrarian questions almost from the beginning of his political career. Both in pre and post independent India he held the opinion that without effectuating revolutionary changes in the agriculture and land system the lot of peasantry would remain miserably poor and deplorable. According to him, "A proper land policy is essential for progress of agriculture."[33] He also argued in favour of abolition of intermediareis, fixation of limit of size of holding and adoption of co-operative farming etc. for the modernisation of Indian agriculture. He started community projects and multi purpose river Valley projects for increasing agriculture and foodgrains production, on May 23, 1956[34] he said in Lok Sabha. "I have no doubt that in the communityproject areas our agricultural production will certainly increase rapidly. On May 07, 1952 at Delhi he stated".[35] I do consider that scheme of community projects is some thing of very great importance. To him, community projects were a source of revolution in the villages and in the hearts of India.[36]

Visionary perspectives essentially reflect the goals and aspirations which people of the country cherish to realise. To Nehru and present policy of LPG both "it is necessary that a vision exercise should first of all capture the nature and the contours of visionary perspectives without tempering them with the considerations of their feasibility in a given time frame. The issues of both the approach Nehrusian and present are to some extent similar :

(i) expansion of per capita income

(ii) achievement of food security

(iii) elimination of poverty

(iv) reduction of inequalities (both internal and external)

(v) removal of infrastructural constraints

(vi) realising growth with stability

(vii) strengthening the knowledge and technology base

(viii) achieving production efficiency at the maximum possible limit

(ix) achieving strong financial sector

(x) restoring values in the society

(xi) ensuring sustainable development

(xii) realising full employment

(xiii) human resource development

(xiv) providing education and health to one and all

(xv) strenthening social security and safety net programme

(xvi) realising optimum water management in the rural and urban economics.

We should not pursue the policy instruments of development, namely globalisation, liberalisation and privatisation as an ends in themselves without critically examining their implications for the cherished goals and aspriations of the common man in the Indian economic society. India is an economy with a very large potential of demand of its population belong to the middle class which has significant demand potential for durable and non-durable goods.

REFERENCES

1. Govt. of India, *Eighth Five Year Plan*, 1992-97, Vol. II, Planning Commission, New Delhi (1992), p. 104.
2. Majumdar, Bhaskar, "*Capitalist Globalisation of the Third World, Compulsions and Choice*", 79th Conference Volume, *The Indian Economic Association* (1996) Gwalior, p. 39. (Quoted from Marx & Engles, 197, p. 46).
3. Chaubey, P.K. Majumdar, B., "*Open Door Industrialisation: A Panacea for the Poor Economy of India*", The Indian Economic Association, Ist April, (Jubilee) 80th Conference Volume, Hyderabad, 1997, p. 455.
4. Singh, Manmohan, *Planning Commission*, 1956, pp. 43-49.
5. Gupta, S.P. (1995), "Important of Economic Reform on Poor", *Economic and Political Weekly*, Vol. XXX, No. 20, June, 1995.
6. Sharma, A.D. (1995), *Economic Reform and Agricultural Policy*, The problem of Rural unemployment, some options, (Seminar on Economic Reform and Agricultural Poilicy, Sardar Patel Institute of Economic & Social Research, Ahmedabad.
7. Datt, Ruddar (1994), "Jobless Growth, Implications of New Economic Policies", *Indian Journal of Industrial Relations*, Vol. 29, No. 4, April, 1995.
8. *Ibid*.
9. *Ibid*.
10. *Annual Conference of Indian National Congress*, Nagpur Session, 1891.

11. *Indian National Congress*, Karanchi Congress, 1937.
12. *Government of India Act*, 1935.
13. Prasad, Permanand, Discussion Regarding Public Enterprises within the Indian National Congress and other Bodies in the Countries.
14. Maheshwari, Neerja, (1977), *Economics of Jawaharlal Nehru*, Deep & Deep Publications, New Delhi, p. 151.
15. *Ibid.*, Quoted from S. Kesava Jyenger.
16. Nehru, Jawaharlal (1962), *Glimpses of World History*, Asia Publishing House, Bombay (2nd Ed.) 1962, p. 239.
17. *Nehru Speeches*, Vol. IV, Speeches in Bangalore, February 6, 1962, p. 150.
18. *Ibid.*, p. 150.
19. *Ibid.*, Vol. IV, *Inaugural Address at the Seminar on Parliamentary Democracy*, New Delhi, December 6, 1957, p. 70.
20. Karanjia, R.K. (1966), *The Philosophy of Mr. Nehru* (As revealed in a series of intimate talks with R.K. Karanjia), George Allen & Unwen, London, 1966, p. 44.
21. *Nehru's Speeches*, Vol. III, Speeches in Trichur, December, 1966, 26, 1955, pp. 136-37.
22. Norman, D. (Ed.) (1955), *Nehru: The First Sixty Years*, Vol. I, Asia Publishing House, New Delhi, Bombay, p. 154.
23. Bright, J.S. (Ed.), *Before and After Independence*, 1922-50, A Collection of Jawaharlal Nehru's Speeches, The Indian Printy Works, New Delhi, p. 124.
24. Nehru, J.L. (1938), *Eighteen Months in India*, Being Further Essays & Writings 1936-37, Kitab Mahal, Allahabad, June 1938, p. 39.
25. Kaushik, P.D. (1964), *Congress Ideology and Programme*, Allied Publishers Pvt. Ltd., Bombay, 1964, p. 158.
26. Brecher, Michael (1969), *Nehru: A Political Biography*, Oxford University Press, London, p. 195.
27. *Ibid.*, p. 196.
28. Desai, P.B. (1979), *Planning in India*, Vikas Publishing House, New Delhi, p. 25.
29. Rao, V.K.R.V. (1968), Planning without Dogma: A Study of Nehru, Rafique Zakaria, A *Times of India* Publication, Bombay, pp. 307-08.

30. *Jawaharlal Nehru's Speeches,* (1949-53), p. 66.
31. *Ibid.,* p. 99.
32. *Ibid.,* Vol. IV, p. 434, Vol. V, pp. 110-16.
33. Independence and After, p. 104.
34. *Ibid.*
25. *Ibid.*
36. *Ibid.*

8

Conclusion

Our first Prime Minister Late Pandit Jawaharlal Nehru was the symbol of hopes and aspirations to the Indian citizen. He was the most loveable friendly, affable, compassionate and forgiving person who respected human digmity. The place of Jawaharlal Nehru in the world history, as one of the foremost statesman of the twentieth century, is well established. He was the first and tallest national leader of our country who adopted a modern outlook to entire aspects of socio-economic national life of our country. He was indeed, an ardent champion of Science and Technology, rationalist of world outlook an advocate of industrialisation and modernisation of Indian economy, a patron of movement for equality, a reformer of social system and a blind supporter of Social Justice.

A man of practical and positive nature and thinking Jawaharlal Nehru was also a man of abstract ideas, this living in two worlds - i.e. 'a world of action' and a world of thought.

The thought developed through intellectual curiosity and the search for knowledge, while action followed a sequence of external events. Man is a part of nature, and also a part of society, and therefore, he has to be nature with nature and human with human society.

Nehru tried to maintain a balance between the two worlds. A childhood without companious, education in a different and distant country, a life in many prisons, and ultimately the office which placed him above others, helped him in varying degrees to live a detacted life. As a nationaist the regarded nationalism as a living force in the history of modern indian economy. How saw in his conception of nationaism not a narrow and fanatical urge but a healthy force. Nationaism is a vital force and Nehru did not want to renounce any part of the genius of the peple or basic traditions.

The study of dynamic life of Jawaharla Nehru is a pleasant and fascinating with his complex personaity. He often presented himself as a paradox and still continues to be an engamatic fegure. He nevertheless steered his socio-economic ideas between the thinking of idealism and realism.

Jawaharlal Nehru was fortunate enough to have been born is a very rich, respectable and aristocratic family at the period of national awakening. His English system of education starting from his early childhood with the English tutors and governess till its ultimate fulfilment through Harrow, Cambridge and London fitted him to be an English aristocrat of Victorian era. But his conversion to socialism with burgenous background is certainly too long a leap.

The thinking of Jawaharlal Nehru was affected by the evil consequences of World War I, the Home Rule Leagued Movement inspired by Lokmanya Tilak and Mrs. Annie Besant, the massacre of Jaliawala Bagh and undespread public movements. This forced him to give up the life of leisure and a jump whole heartedly into the national movement for freedom. The political life of Nehru actually began from here.

Jawaharlal Nehru was the product of Indian renaissance and revolution to which he was to give snape and content the emerged from Gandhi Era.[1]

Jawaharlal Nehru was never a student of Economics

which was not a popular subject of his time. He was a Science Student at Cambridge but his interest was attracted by social science. He was totally ignorant of labour condition in factories and fields and the laws of economic tendencies till 1920.[2] With his active participation in the freedom struggle gradually he "came into an intemete touch with the realities of economic situation. The peasants who took away his shyness, incidently gave him currage to express his ideas and feelings before the public.[3]

As Dadabhai Naoroji and Gopal Krishna Gokhale were the nation's tribunes. Gandhi and Jawaharlal Nehru became "their heirs". They would not have been if they had not been.[4] He had immense faith in the leadership of Gandhi Ji which had a "surprisingly solid man-base. The victory of Gandhi Ji and adventures in Champaran filled young Jawaharlal with extreme" enthusiasm[5] which promised a successful future before him. In encouraging the mind of Nehru as is obvious from his own words. Sarojini Naidu played an equally significant role." I remember being moved by a number eloquent speeches by Sarojini Naidu. It was all nationalism and patriolism and I was pure nationalist my vague socialist ideas of college days having sunk into the background."[6]

He became convinced by his European tour during March 1926 and December 1927 that without social freedom and a socialistic structure of society and state neither the country nor the individual could develop much." The writings of Karl Marx impressed him much and lightened up many a dark corner of his mind, history had new interpretation for him and" communist philosophy" gave him comfort and hope."[7]

Gandhian approach was not early understood and it was estimated wrong by him many times. Consequently, he fell it quite unreal.[8] But he actually derived the main stream of inspirations from the economic philosophy of Gandhi Ji and felt that Gandhi's Socialism" was certainly an alternative to the "Laisser-Faire competitive Industrialism" in its end" although the 'means' were to provide a congenial background for the growth of socialism.[9]

At this stage the developed interest in "Utopian Socialism" and not in Scientific socialism" and even this was all very academic.[10] Probably his interest was due to a vegue feeling that in such socialist ideologies there was implied idea of "anti-colomialism."[11]

The economic fluctuations taught him the true nature of the economy and he felt that the political freedom was an absolute necessity to curb such cycles to utilise "surplus man power and unexploited natural resources, he pondered that the State of affairs were probably due to the stagnancy of techniques, which inhabited socio-economic factors and prevented growth and development, socialistic planning in Soviet Russia offered one solution to his awakening of the economic situation and problem in the country.[12] He found that equality and freedom were the basic arguments against imperialism or capitalism, and "they remained the basic arguments against poverty, ignorance and disease and socialism could be a means to achieve a classless society, where equalisation of wealth, opportunity and social justice could be attained forcibly."[13] Jawaharlal Nehru became an ardent admirer of Socialism but he disliked force and was not prepared to brook dictatorship of any kind either of capital or of proletariat.[14]

The socialist learnings of Jawaharlal Nehru were not purely economic but cultural and ethical too.[15] This aimed at moral, cultural and economic revolution togethe. He regarded class struggle as inevitable for social revolution and never suffered from the delussion that moral appeals for Justice will be so responded by dominant classes that they would voluntarily agree to the lequidation of domination and exploitation.[16] He accepted the principle of class collaboration. The dominating spirit of his social ideas was almost similar to that of Gandhiji's". He set down his thoughts more systematically.[17] In western terms he emerged as a "felt-Socialist" of the "Austrian School," Maraxist in theory, democratic in practice. According to him such a democratic socialism could only be achieved by systematised and conscious efforts in the form of national planning. Besides planning could be significant only with great deal of state control.

The various of Nehru were the outcome of the typical circumstances prevailing in the pre-independence era which held him responsible an a primary architect of national building. Being impressed by the valiance, vigilance and vigour of Jawaharlal,[18] Gandhi magnamimously gave way to him. He accepted the idea of decentralised village industries but only to a limited extent and as a subsidiary past of national economy.[19] He firmly believed that if industrialisation is socialised, it would be free from the basic evils of capitalism as the state ownership will eradicate them, and trusteeship will be built.

His life was subline and drew aside the veil of darkness from our lives to let us live in eternal sunrise. He was a great historian of his time. He read history, wrote history, made history, taught history and created a historical vision for Independent India.

He was deeply touched by the depressed people and wanted to find solution to fight the poverty sticking to higher percentage of British Indians. As such, creation of new dimensions for economic development became strong basis for him. His deepest urges sprang from his love for his nation. He wanted to review the prestige of the past as he was enamoured by the vast potential and natural resources of British India, which were mysteriously drained out for the benefit of outlandish people. Nehru learnt the treat of economic development of Mughal and British Indian History, he carefully studied the socio-economic structure of pre-British India and British influences over it. He did not shink from reading the economic thought of eighteenth and early nineteenth centuries analysed the pross and coins of different scholastic views, his early youth was consumed mainly in observing the nature of British Indian economy and response of the people.

Jawaharlal Nehru read the socialists theories and was captivated by the achievement of Soviet Union and was distinctly influenced by the views of Karl Marx but was not absolute agreement with his ideas. He realised that Marx possessed an extra-ordinary insight into the social phenomenon due to his scientific approach. He travelled far and wide the Soviet Union and was impressed not only by the magnitude of the progress but the change which the revolution had brought about the State of the people. He was equally influenced by the willingness of the Soviet Unbion to extend assistance without attracting strings to developing countries in their efforts to transforma colonial into a national economy. His economic thought formulated a silent pattern of socialism.

Nehru was equally anamoured by Gandhiji, his socialistic views and his hypotism towards the Indian masses, brought a revelation and revolution in his life and outlook, that he tookout the bourgeous covering of his personality and became an ardent socialist. His sacrifice was greater than Mahatma Gandhi as he came from an aristocratic background and resented as advertisement of poverty. He developed a sense of prestige to be Indian but not poor.

His economic ideology developed a long way towards building a self-reliant, modern economy to make its political freedom secure and meaningful to the vast masses of the people.

His socio-economic ideas are still relevant useful and

meaningful even at the age of globalisation, liberalisation, privatisation and economic reform.

This study is an attempt for the monitoring and evaluation of main socio-economic ideas of Jawaharlal Nehru in the economic reform and globalisation especially in the new millenium. The first chapter of the book contains introduction of the subject, while second chapter deals with main economic ideas of Jawaharlal Nehru. A comprehensive and analytical study has been made on his economic ideas consisting of laissez-faire doctrine, its main objectives importance, evils, profit-motive free enterprise pig philosophy, democracy in laissez-faire policy, economic function of the State Capitalism meaning form, objectives, merits and demerits, profit motive, worker's position, paradox, failures of capitalism, socio-economic structure, conditions of poor consumers, evil-effects, democracy and capitalism and relevance of capitalism, agriculture, land reform measures, rural development, development of infrastructure, co-operative farming industrialisation, role problems of cottage and small scale industries, new economic order, capital formation, pattern of taxation, stages of economic growth population problem and family planning etc.

The third chapter consists of main social ideas of Jawaharlal Nehru meaning of socialism, relationship between socialism and capitalism, socialistic pattern of society, its main role merits and demerits, dimension, growth, role sociolistic views on problem of production and distribution, industrial revolution, problems of inequality, exploitation, poverty, regional imbalance, unemployment, social unjustice, difference between socialistic pattern of society etc. have carefully been examined especially in terms of new millenium.

The fourth chapter attempts to review the ideas of Jawaharlal Nehru on public sector in a critical, comprehensive and analytical manner. He was the greatest advocate of public sector. He formulated and announced Industrial policy Resolution 1956 the so called 'Industrial Constitution of India.' He examined carefully and properly the needs, objectives, merits demerits, role, accountability autonomy and control of public sector. He argued that without public sector India cannot fulfil its various socio-economic achievements. Public sector occupies key role in our socio-economic activities and has proved to be the most vital part of our economy even today. It is an engine of growth for social justice. It is highly essential for the creation of enormous employment opportunities, optimum utilisation of available resources, social sector, promotion of balanced regional development. He classified public accountability of public enterprises as parliamentary, ministerial and audit accountability. He played key role in enforcing parliamentary questions, debates and parliamentary committees i.e. Public Accounts Committee Estimates Committee and Committee on Public Undertaking with the help and kind co-operation of the Speaker Mr. G.V. Mavlankar and the member of Parliaments particularly Mr. Lanka Sundaram in monitoring the performance of public sector undertaking in India.

The fifth chaper illustrates Jawaharlal Nehru and planning. To Pandit Nehru, planning is a logical, scientific and organised approach to an objective of national building. He accepted planning 'as a grand panacea of our age.' It was something like ladder by which one may goes up from one step to another. It was a system of organisation of all activities, production distribution and consumption. His approach towards planning was pragmatic and practical. He had long been personally interated in economic planning. He deeply studied the economic planning by Soviet Russia and also visited several places. He played very significant role in the formation and execution of Indian Planning i.e. development of Bombay Plan of 1944. People's plan of Mr. M.N. Roy. The Gandhian Planning, Planning Commission and he National

Development Council and introduced in Five Year Plans respectively in Indian economy. In 1946, he set up a Planning Advisory Board and Economic Programme Committee in the Interim Government.

Economic planning, as an instrument of development, was adopted in India in 1951 by Jawaharlal Nehru. During the pre-Independence period a few unofficial development plans were prepared at the initiative of both the national leaders and the leading industrialists of the country. There plans, however, could not be put into practice on account of indifference of the British rulers to India's development needs. The significance of these plans was, thus, merely historical as they reflected the aspirations of the people during the late British period and the way and means which they wanted to follow for realising their objectives.

The pioneering work from this points of view was done by the National Planning Committee under the Chairmanship of Jawaharlal Nehru. All these plans were completely ignored by the Government for obvious reasons. Nonetheless they created a consciousness towards economic planning which later on influenced the actual planning process in the country.

India's Independence paved the way for the adoption of economic planning. Nehru broadly stated the principal objectives of economic planning as to achieve.

(a) rapid economic growth

(b) self-reliance

(c) full employment

(d) modernisation

(e) social justice

(f) economic growth with stability; and

(g) price stability

Off all the long term objectives of economic planning in Indian economic growth has always been given the greatest attention by the Nehru Govt. He alongwith other planners assumed that the realisation of other objectives is very much linked with the realisation of the growth objectives. But our own experience in this country over the past five decades clearly shows that the gains of economic growth do not automatically percolate downwards and thus, special measures are required to take unemployment, poverty regional embalances, price fluctuations etc.

The sixth chapter broadly examines Jawaharlal Nehru and parliament. As obvious Nehru has been recognised as the architect of modern India and modern parliamentary democracy, true democrat, master builder of parliamentary system, his respect to parliamentary democracy and institution and presiding officers such as Speaker of Lok Sabha and Chairman & Dy. Chairman of the Rajya Sabha and his attitudes and relations with the leader of the opposition in both the House of the Parliament. He had abiding faith in parliamentary system. He firmly desired that parliamentarians should offer their opinions freely without fear and favour. He gave great attention towards opposition in the Parliament.

Throughout his tenure of office as Prime Minister and Leader of the House, he regarded himself as the Principal gardian of the rights of Parliament. He found enough time to give to the work of both the Rajya Sabha and Lok Sabha. His faith in the parliamentary system was obiding and deep rooted. Speaking as a seminar in December, 1957 at Delhi, he said, we praise the parliamentary form of government because it is a peaceful method of dealing with problems, it is a method of argument, discussion and decision, and of accepting that decision, even through we may not agree with it." He believed that the parliamentary system, with all its failings has the virtue that it can fit in with the changing pattaern of fire to him, the will of parliament was beyond the question. The sovereign will of people found true expression in parliament. The Prime Minister's presence lent special significance to the proceedings, besides ensuring a near full House. During the parliamentary sessions Nehru would keep himself in constant touch with the proceedings and would walk into either House.

Nehru welcomed criticism in Parliament. Criticism drew from him the best in his parliamentary skills. To him, parliament's business was serious. He kept himself close touch with Members of Parliament both ruling party and opposition their moods and their vagaries. As the founder of the world's biggest parliamentary democracy, Nehru had raised the image of India to the highest pinnacle of glory. He enriched parliamentary democracy by the high standard.

The seventh chapter relates to the studies of socio-economic ideas of Jawaharlal Nehru in new economic reform and globalisation in relation to the new millennium. As obvious from this chapter, his socio-economic ideas are very useful in terms of even liberalisation, globalisation, privatisation and economic reform duly launched in 1991 in India. Globalisation, implies a regime of competitive markets with no entry or exist barrier. Globalisation in the profened goal of the on-going economic reform. Industrial policy reform, trade policy exchange control reform financial sector reform, public sector enterprise reform, capital market reform and increased direct foreign investment are directly and indirectly related to his ideas. His ideas of profit maximisation, industrialisation, location of plants, cheap labour policy, laisez faire strategiess. ISI strategies and liberalisation, profit motive, incentives, individual freedom, mixed economy, capitalism, poverty, unemployment alleviation, agricultural and land reform, rural development, capital formation, trade and commerce, economic order, public finance, planning, education, health, public sector, social welfare, social security measures, population policy, cottage and small scale industries, khadi industries, co-operative movement etc. have found very significant place in the present period of globalisation and liberalisation. The Nobel Prize winner during 1998 Prof. Amartya Sen has also supported the move of globalisation particularly at this juncture alongwith Nehruvian model.

Several Third World Nations including India are passing through a rather difficult and painful transition. The package of economic reforms constitutes a sharp turn around in policy thinking compared to the licence-permit raj built up during 1960's & 1970's. The main purpose of globalisation and Jawaharlal Nehru's socio-economic ideas has been to make India economicallystrong stable, self-reliant and economic and political freedom more relevant and meaningful. His ideas have all directed towards laying a strong foundation of settered economy of India. The deviation from the thinking and ideas of Jawaharlal Nehru in present global perspective has also resulted insufficient production, unequal distribution and unstable economic and political situation. His concept of economic freedom included an economic structure based on economic equality on the well-being of the masses and on co-operative spirit. His idea of an egaliterian society was a co-operative ideal based on social justice and economic equality. His economic freedoom is the central point of economic reform and globalisation whose main aim is to reduce the gap between the favoured few and unfavoured millions. After completion of decade of globalisation and liberalisation a critical comparative and analytical analysis has compelled every body to give top priority to Nehruvian models alongwith economic reforms and globalisation for sustainable, balanced economic growth and stronger ceremony and to achieve socio-economic and welfare in the new millennium. Nehruvian ideas are still quite relevant and useful. These can't be overlooked and neglected in India and other developing nations. Nehruvian ideas compell policy-makers to rethink the role of state in the new millennium.

Findings

To sum up:

1. He did not panic over excessive number on agriculture.
2. He believed that in order to stabilise the food economy and to ensure an adequate return to the farmers all trade in foodgrains will have to be gradually institutionalised.
3. He formulated his policy on assumption that in feudal economy agrticultural production could be expanded in two ways:

   (i) through organisational & institutional changes and

   (ii) through increased and improved inputs which would make there changes fruitful and effective.
4. his agricultural policy sought to promote two parallel revolutions:

   (i) agrarian revolution

   (ii) technological revolution
5. His land reform policy recognised that it had rural purpose to play:

   (a) to ensure increased productivity and

   (b) elimination of exploitation.

   Consequently, legislatious were passed in a number of staes for converting tenants and sub-tenants into owners.
6. He launched co-operative movement particularly co-operative farming as encourages cohesion among the village people and performs many functions in addition

to providing credit. To him, through co-operatives the villagers shall perform many things which now they perform individually. Co-operative may give them strength and help farmers to produce more and adopt new and more remunerative methods of agriculture.

7. He was of the view that small co-operatives comprising for two or three village, should not be controlled from above not too afficiatised but should present the spirit of self-reliance, and self growth of the people.

   This whole movement, as our entire political and economic structure in India must be conditioned by democratic process.

8. Community Development in India has arrived at a crucial stage. Community movement must now pass progressively to the people.

9. To him, future pattern of agrarian economy must rest for pillars namely.

   (a) it should provide an opportunity for the development of the personality of farmers.

   (b) there should be no scope for the exploitation of one class by another.

10. He deemed co-operation a forceful instrument for bringing about equality in the distribution of income and wealth, socio-economic justice materialising socialistic ideas into practice and ultimately building India a new.

11. He classified that he has a socialist and a Republican. Socialism does not kill or supress individuality.

12. He was convinced that only socialism can solve the problems of India and the world.

13. He believed in decolonisation and racial equality with cultural efflorescence. He recognised Marshall's social

possibilities of economic chivatry that he assumed that poor have a claim over rich.

14. He felt that the economic development could be facilated through foreign assistance in the form of men, material and money.

15. The roots of his socialism were spreading and enlarging for peace and internationalism.

16. His socialism could mean that economic side of the democratic ideal. He wished his people to acquire energy and the strength to endure and suffer.

17. He stood for a mixed economy which was to a great extent socialistic but he was not Marxist. His socialistic ideal implied 'planned production and its equitable distribution which was to be inculculated legitimately and peaceful.

18. His action programme included land reforms, equitable distribution of income and wealth, development of cottage and small scale industries and friendly relations between capital and labour.

19. His economic policy became progressive. It cornered socialism in wide sense and conscience of planning for sheping India's destinty.

20. He believed that socialism was not only a system of socio-economic organisation but something deeper which involves a way of thing and living. Socialism is based on the growth of material resources as well as social justice and co-operative method of works.

21. He did never advocate socialisation or nationalisation of all means of production distribution and exchange. He favoured controls rather than ownership.

22. He was the pioneer in sponsoring a modern outlook

for restructing and reconstructing the set up of Indian economy.

23. He considered his thought on democratic planning as a new experiment for would/global economic order.

24. In order to avoid evils he argued that it was not industrialism which had to be given up but industrial development has to be planned on socialistic lines.

25. He championed the cause of science and modern higher productive technology as a means to an end the good life for the masses.

26. He wanted to build up swaraj right from the village with adequate and necessary powers, functions and resources.

27. He favoured quality of man as the new economic order. It is the quality of human being that counts in life and builds up the wealth of nation.

28. He was in favour of progressive taxation and principle of ability to pay.

29. He deeply and widely probed the problem of capital formation in developing economies like India. He wanted to finance economic development schemes through taxation, internal public debt and defict financing. But he disfavoured deficit financing beyond limit, he often said that foreign borrowing involves a slight risk.

30. Population problem was considered as a global problem by him which directly comes in a way to the process of economic development which keeps the standard of living quite low besides, tremendous growth of population in eating up resources of the world at a terrific pace. He as such advocated amily planning as an official policy.

31. To him, take-off stage can't take place at the very commencement of economic development in a stegnant economy.

32. He described conflict between capitalism and democracy as inherent and continuous.

33. He strongly stressed as the development of infrastructural facilities i.e.

34. He was against prompt motive though, he advocated for incentives.

35. He was against unplanned enterprise and opposed concentration of wealth in the individual hands.

36. He made capitalism partly wrong and a partly right. He admitted that failure of capitalism and proclaimed that industrial revolution and capitalism can solve the problem of production but can't solve the problem of distribution of wealth.

37. His ideas of agriculture and land reform still form the basis of Indian economy and are very useful.

38. He observed that every farmer should only as much land as he and his family are able to cultivate to him, Zamindars were the middle men stood between cultivators and state. Government should do more and more for the cultivators and kisans.

    He advocated for the adoption of Japanese farm models consting of small and marginal farmers and the mechanisation of agriculture and abolition of zamindary system.

    He accepted that the reforms have a pecular significance and he considered it more scientific and revolutionary and initiated a number of notable steps for the welfare of the cultivators.

39.(a) Like Robbins he described "Planning as the grand panacea of our age" and considered it as a sovereign remedy for all economic ills.

(b) He considered efficiency in production and equality in distribution as the main objectives of planning. Consequently, economic, social and political motives combine in the formation of the objectives of planning.

(c) A good plan must provide a strategy for economic advances.

(d) To ensure economic stability in developed countries and to accelerate economic growth in developing economies are the central and fundamental objectives of economic planning.

(e) The strategy of planning has to be changed according to the changing economic situation or according to the uregently of the problems that a country may have to face and tackle.

40. According to Nehru United Nation publication mentioned following aims and objectives of planning i.e.

(i) a diversified economy.

(ii) a rapid increase in per capita income.

(iii) a reduction of inequalities in income distribution.

(iv) a relatively stable price level.

(v) a high level of employment.

(vi) equilibrem in the balance of payment; and

(vii) the avoidance of market disparities.

41. The objective of economic planning in India according

to Nehru is the establishment of a socialistic pattern of society in which socio-economic disparities reduced to the minimum.

42. He focussed attention on rapid industrialisation which is the hallmark of the modern development.

43. He said "the good of planned development in under-developed countries is the establishment ultimately of an egalitarian society or socialism. "Philosophy of socialism has gradually permitted the entire structure of the society word over and almost the only points in dispute are the pace and the methods of advance of its full realisation.

It is rather impossible to recount all the socio-economic achievement of Nehru in one piece. He was not truncated social scientist concerned only about demand and supply of goods and services or any other sources and allocation of national income. He took a higher view and meaning of economic activities. He would have accepted the failure of state as a producer of goods and services. He would have supported capitalism in production and socialism in distribution. Though a man of quick temper, he was honestly scientific enough to review his views and modify them if they were at variance with reality. Intellectually integrity and external values were an obsession with him, and thus to my mind is his final message to all of us who have inherited legacy. He examined the relation of economic activityto the end of all human activity.

The principle of economy which has so far been accepted as the guiding criterian of economic activity should, therefore, be subjected to the following qualifications:

(a) satisfaction of the minimum economic requirements of all the individuals in the community.

(b) encouragement by subsidies, bounties, tariffs or other

means of those types of economic activity which field a social marginal not product larger than their marginal private net product, and discouragement by taxes quotas and other means of those types of economic activities which yield the opposite results,

(c) full employment of labour,

(d) scope or play of creative instinct,

(e) absence of personality killing element and,

(f) character formation.

While international aid is both crucial and important, the major determinant of India's economic growth will be the quality, discipline and dedication of Indian leadership. Once the economic take-off is completed, incentives can be permitted more freedom of operation. In the final analysis the Indian challenge of reconciling economic development with democratic freedom can only be answered on Indian soil with Indian resources by the efforts of the Indian people. It may be suggested that a more useful purpose will be served of direct comparisons of real income are attempted by comparative feagures of consumption, productivity and the like instead of resorting to national income totals. There is indeed a need to adopt a far more positive and studied approach to the productive use of human factor in Indian economy.

He, as such, covered all most all the crucial areas in Economics and Social Science and his contribution to practical Economics & Social Science and enormous. He was of the firm opinion that economic principles will not get us the desired results unless there is the sense of belonging across each and every segment of society. The observation made by Jawaharlal Nehru in this connection is worth quoting: "What is needed is a firm and clear policy by government, understanding and co-operation from the public, spirited action by our producers conscience from traders and commitment from the workers.

He believed mixed economy for the rapid economic development through the joint efforts of private and public sector. The strategy suggested by Jawaharlal Nehru is called cluster approach for micro regional planning which promoted horizontal linkage between neighbouring villages by cementing inter-connectivity between villages both for production as well as distribution of growth between villages, particularly weaker sections of the society for eliminating income inequalities through promotion of required skills for the spatial development of rural areas.

His approach of making villages and villagers self-sufficient avoiding exploitative sucking tendency of urban areas from villages. This will avoid drain of resources from villages to towns and use them fully for the benefit of rapid development of rural areas by bring about functional and national integration of the backward villages by promoting positive and profitable inter-connectivity. His main purpose was to develop agricultural activities fully and link them with non-agricultural activities in villages by maximum utilisation of their resources and skills or promoting and providing rural welfare equatably so as to achieve growth with justice by enlighting both rich and poor sections in rural areas for achieving maximum welfare by their active participation.

REFERENCES

1. Rao, N. Chalapath (1967), *Gandhi and Nehru,* Third Publishers, Bombay, p. 51.
2. Venkateshwaran, R.J. (1962), *The Impact of Jawaharlal Nehru on Indian Economy,* Oxford Book Company, Calcutta, p. 3.
3. Mooraes, Frank (1959), *Jawaharlal Nehru,* Jaicob Publishing House, Bombay, p. 69.
4. Gandhi, B.N. (1977), *Indian Economic Thought,* Nineteenth Century, Tata McGraw Hill Publishing Co., New Delhi, Perspective Chapter 12 "Political Economy in the world" of Gandhi & Nehru, p. 239, 1977.

5. Gupta, Padmini Sen, (1966), *Sarojini Naidu: A Biography*, Asia Publishing House, New Delhi, 1966, p. 115.

6. Lane, John, (1936), *Jawaharlal Nehru: An Autobiography*, The Bodley Head, London, 1936, p. 35.

7. Venkateshwaran, R.J. (1962), *op. cit.*, pp. 2-3.

8. Bishnudayal B. (1975), *Mahatama Gandhi: A New Approach*, Bhartiya Vidya Bhawan, Bombay, 1975, p. 3.

9. Prasad, Rai Akhilendra, (1974), *Socialist Through in Modern India*, Meenakshi Prakashan, Meerut, 1974, p. 18.

10. Menda, Tiber, (1958), *Conversation with Nehru*, Wilco Publishing House, Bombay, 1958, p. 13.

11. *Ibid.*

12. Radica, Giles (1965), *Democratic Socialism*, Longmans Green & Co. Ltd., 1965, The Developing World, pp. 138-39.

13. Kaushik, P.D. (1964), *Congress Ideology and Programme*, Allied Publishers Pvt. Ltd., Bombay, 1964, p. 122.

14. Singh, V.B. (1977), *Nehru on a Socialism Government of India*, Publication Division, March 1977, Delhi, preface, p. V.

15. Gopel, Sarvapalli, (1976), *Jawaharlal Nehru*, Vol. I, 1889-1947, Oxford University Press, Bombay, 1976, p. 66.

16. Government of India, (1957), *Jawaharlal's Speeches*, 1949-53, Ministry of Information and Broadcasting Division, Second Impression, 1957, p. 411.

17. Jawaharlal & Jagdish Prasad, Chief Secretary, U.P. 11th March to Maharaj Singh Commissioner, Allahabad Division 9th April, 1931, Home Deptt. Pol. File 33/XVI & K.W. of 1931.

18. Brecher; Mithael, (1965), *Nehru: A Political Biography*, Oxford University Press, London, 1969, p. 81.

19. Norman, Dorothy, (1965), *Nehru The First Sixty Years*, Asia Publishing House, Bombay, 1965, p. 115.

Bibliography

Books

1. Nehru, Jawaharlal (1936): *An Autobiography*, (Bodley Head), London.
2. Nehru, Jawaharlal (1934-35): *Glimpses of World History*, 2 Vols. (Kitabistan), Allahabad.
3. Nehru, Jawaharlal (1946): *Discovery of India*, (Signet Press) Calcutta, (Ist Ed.), Meridian Books Ltd., London.
4. Nehru, Jawaharlal (1930): *Letters from A Father of His Daughter*, (1st Ed.), (Kitabistan), Allahabad.
5. Nehru, Jawaharlal (1946-49): *Collection of Speeches*, Vol. I (Publication Division), Government of India, New Delhi.
6. Nehru, Jawaharlal (1949-53): *Ibid.*, Vol. II.
7. Nehru, Jawaharlal (1953-57): *Ibid.*, Vol. III.
8. Nehru, Jawaharlal (1957-63): *Ibid.*, Vol. IV.
9. Nehru, Jawaharlal (1936): *Recent Essays and Writings on Future of India, Commercial and other Subjects*, (Kitabistan), Allahabad, Vol. I.
10. Nehru, Jawaharlal (1936): *Essays II: India and The World* (George Allen and Unwin Ltd.), London.
11. Nehru, Jawaharlal (1936-37): *Eighteen Months in India* (Kitabistan), Allahabad, Vol. III.

12. Nehru, Jawaharlal (1948): *Writing I, Nehru, Jawaharlal: The Unity of India,* (Lindsay, Drumond), London.

13. Nehru, Jawaharlal (1950): *Writing II, Selected Writing of Jawaharlal Nehru,* 1916-50 (ed.) J.S. Bright, *The Indian Printing Works,* New Delhi.

14. Nehru, Jawaharlal (1954): *Speeches I, Independence and After* (A collection of more important speeches of Jawaharlal Nehru from September 1946 to May 1949) (Ministry of Information and Broadcasting), Government of India.

15. Nehru, Jawaharlal (1955): *Speeches II, Speeches of Jawaharlal Nehru,* 1949-53.

16. Nehru, Jawaharlal (1958): *Speeches III,* (March 1953 - Aug. 1957).

17. Nehru, Jawaharlal (1958): *Constituent Assembly Debates* (Lok Sabha Secretariat), New Delhi.

18. Nehru, Jawaharlal (1960): *Legislative Debates* (Constituent Assembly of India), Lok Sabha Secretariat, New Delhi.

19. Nehru, Jawaharlal (1962): *Parliamentary Debates,* Parliament of India, *Ibid.*

20. Nehru, Jawaharlal (1958): *Letters: A Bunch of Old Letters,* (Written monthly to Jawaharlal Nehru & some written by him).

21. Nehru, Jawaharlal (1951): *Talks: Talks with Nehru,* A Discuss between Nehru and Norman Cousin, London.

22. Nehru, Jawaharlal (1956): *Conversations,* Conservations with Nehru by Tibor Mende (Seeker and Warbung), London, 1956.

23. Nehru, Jawaharlal (1954): *Press Conference,* 1950-54, (India Information Service), New Delhi.

24. Nehru, Jawaharlal (1950): Visit to America, New York.

25. Nehru, Jawaharlal (1940): *China, Spain and the War,* (Kitabistan), Allahabad.

26. Nehru, Jawaharlal (1933): *Prisan Land,* (Kitabistan), Allahabad.

27. Nehru, Jawaharlal (1937): *The Question of Language,* (Kitabistan), Allahabad.

28. Nehru, Jawaharlal (1955): Letters to the P.C.C. President, New Delhi.

29. Nehru, Jawaharlal (1955): *Towards a Socialistic Order,* New Delhi.

30. Nehru, Jawaharlal (1956): *Planning and Development,* Delhi.

31. Nehru, Jawaharlal (1959): *Youth's Blunder,* Bombay.

32. Nehru, Jawaharlal (1959): *Nehru visit U.S.A.* Washington.

33. Nehru, Jawaharlal (1959): *On Community Development,* Delhi.

34. Agrawal, S. Narayan (1959): *Towards a Socialist Economy,* New Delhi.

35. Apsler, Alfred (1963): *Jawaharlal Fighter for Independence Julian,* Messuer, New York.

36. Anthony, Frank (1986): *Nehru and Secular Democracy,* Lok Sabha Secretariat, New Delhi.

37. Adisheshiah, A. 1994: "Foreign Investment and Liberalisation", *Yojna,* Vol. 38, No. 12, August 15.

38. Baur, P.T. (1961): *Indian Economic Policy and Development* (George Allen and Unwin), London.

39. Bishnudayal, B. (1975): *Mahatma Gandhi: A New Approach* (Bhartiya Vidya Bhawan), Bombay.

40. Bright, J.S. (1922-50): (Ed.) *Before and After Independence, Speeches Delivered by Jawaharlal Nehru,* New Delhi.

41. Baig, Tara Ali (1986): *Nehru and Democracy* (Lok Sabha Secretariat), New Delhi.

42. Chablan (1961): *Motilal Nehru* (S. Chand & Co.), Delhi.

43. Ahluwalia, B.K. (1967): (Ed.) *Facts of Nehru,* (S.E.S. Company), New Delhi.

44. Brecher, Michael (1969): *Nehru: A Political Biography,* (Oxford University, Press), London.

45. Bajpai, Nirupan (1995): "Economic Reforms in Developing Countries: Theory and Evidence", *(EPW)* Vol. 3, No. 14, Bombay.

46. Cousins, Norman (1951): *Talks with Nehru,* John Day, New York.

47. Chatterjee, Bishwajeet (1977): *Globalisation of Indian Economy, The TashkAhead* OCCASIONAL PAPERS, vol. 5, Rabindra Bharti University, Calcutta, March.

48. Chhiber (1970): *Jawaharlal Nehru,* Vikas Publication, Delhi.

49. Desai, P.B. (1979): *Planning in India* (Vikas Publication), New Delhi.

50. Das, K.B. (1991): *Regional Economic Development and Decentralisation,* Discovery Publication House, New Delhi.

51. Dutta Ruddar (1996): *Economic Reforms in India: A Critique,* S. Chand & Co., New Delhi.

52. Diwakar R.R. (1986): *Nehru and Parliamentary*

Democratic: Some Thoughts, Lok Sabha Secretariate, New Delhi.

53. Das, A.N. (1980): *Nehru's Vision of Parliamentary Democracy.*

54. Ebenstein (1970): *Modern Political Thought,* Oxford University Press & I.B.H., New Delhi, 1970.

55. Ganguli, B.N. (1977): *Indian Economic Thought Nineteenth Century Perspective.*

56. Gopal Ram (1962): *The Trails of Jawaharlal Nehru,* Book Centre, New Delhi.

57. Gupta, S.P. (1995): "Economic Reforms & Its Impact on the Poor", *Economic and Political Weekly,* June 1995.

58. Grover, Virendra (1988): *Jawaharlal Nehru,* Deep & Deep Publication, New Delhi.

59. Gangadeb (1986): *Nehru as the Leader of the Lok Sabha* (Lok Sabha Secretariate), New Delhi.

60. Gurupadswamy, M.S. (1986): *Nehru as I Saw* (Lok Sabha Secretariate), New Delhi.

61. Gandhi, M.K. (1930): *Harijan,* 27 May, 1930.

62. Hutheesing, Krishna (1963): *Nehru's Letters to His Sister* (Feber and Feber, London, 1963).

63. Gopal S. (1980): *The Mind of Jawaharlal Nehru* (Sangam Books, Orient Longmais), Madras, 1980.

64. Husain S. Abid (1959): *The War of Gandhi and Nehru,* Bombay, 1959.

65. Kurein, C.J. (1969): Indian Economic Crisis (Asia Publication House), Bombay.

66. Kapoor, P. (1990): *Economic Thought of Jawaharlal Nehru* (Deep & Deep Publication), New Delhi.

67. Kothari, R. (1995): "Globalisation & New World Order: What further for the United Nation?" *Economic & Political Weeklky*, Aug.

68. Kidwai, Anser (1986): *Nehru and Working Democracy* (Lok Sabha Secretariate), New Delhi.

69. Khan, R. (1986): *Nehru as a Democrat* (Lok Sabha Secretariate), New Delhi.

70. Krishnamurthi, Y.G. (1944): *Jawaharlal Nehru: The Man and His Ideas* (Popular Book Depot.), Bombay, 1944.

71. Karanjia, R.K. (1966): *The Philosophy of Mr. Nehru*, Allen & Unwin, London, 1966.

72. Kripalani, K.R. (1949): *Gandhi, Tagore and Nehru*, Bombay.

73. Kamraj, K. and others (1966): *The Nehru Legacy* (National Book Club Publication), New Delhi, 1966.

74. Kaushik, P.D. (1964): *Congress Ideology and Programme* (Allied Publishers Pvt. Ltd.), Bombay.

75. Moraes, Frank (1959): *Jawaharlal Nehru*, Jaicab Publishing House, Bombay.

76. Mende, Tiber (1958): *Conversation with Nehru*, Wilco Publishing House, Bombay.

77. Mehta Ashok (1969): *Social Justice and National Development* (Popular Prakashan), Bombay, 1969.

78. Mehta, Ashok (1959): *Studies in Asian Socialism* (Akhil Bhartiya Serva Seva Sangh Prakashan), Kashi.

79. Khan, R. (1986): *Nehru as a Democrat* (Lok Sabha Secretariate), New Delhi.

80. Krishnamurthi, Y.G. (1944): *Jawaharlal Nehru: The Man and His Ideas* (Popular Book Depot), Bombay, 1944.

81. Karanjia, R.K. (1966): *The Philosophy of Mr. Nehru,* Allen & Unwin, London, 1966.

82. Kripalani, K.R. (1949): *Gandhi, Tagore and Nehru,* Bombay.

83. Kamraj, K. & others (1966): *The Nehru Legacy* (National Book Club Publication), New Delhi, 1966.

84. Kaushik, P.D. (1964): *Congress Ideology and Programme* (Allied Publishers Pvt. Ltd.), Bombay.

85. Moraes, Frank (1959): *Jawaharlal Nehru* (Jaicab Publishing House), Bombay.

86. Mende, Tiber (1958): *Conversation with Nehru,* Wilco Publishing House, Bombay.

87. Mehta, Ashok (1969): *Social Justice and National Development* (Popular Prakashan), Bombay, 1969.

88. Mehta, Ashok (1959): *Studies in Asian Socialism* (Akhil Bhartiya Serva Seva Sangh Prakashan), Kashi.

89. Martein G.C. (1962): *India's First Prime Minister* (Black & Sons Ltd.), Bombay.

90. Malviya, H.D. (1961): *Jawaharlal Nehru Congressmen, Premier for Socialism* (Orient Longman's), New Delhi.

91. Myrdal, Gunnar (1968): *Asian Drama* (In 3 Vol.), (Pelican Books), 1968.

92. Malvankar, G.V. (1961): *Speeches And Writings* (Lok Sabha Secretariate), New Delhi.

93. Mehta, Krishna (1986): *Nehru and Opposition* (Lok Sabha Secretariate), New Delhi.

94. Mukherjee Pranab (1986): *Nehru and Rajya Sabha* (Lok Sabha Secretariate).

95. Mukherjee, Pranab (1986): *Beyond Survival* (Vikas Publication), New Delhi.

96. Marak, R.R. (1986): *The Father of Parliamentary Democracy* (Lok Sabha Secretariate), New Delhi.

97. Mahtab, Karekrishna (1986): *Architect of Parliamentary Democracy in India, Ibid.*

98. Maheshwari, N. (1997): *Economic Policy of Jawaharlal Nehru* (Deep & Deep Publication), New Delhi.

99. Mishra, O.P. (1978): *The Economic Philosophy of Jawaharlal Nehru* (Chugh Publication), Allahabad.

100. Norman Dorothy (1965): *Nehru: The First Sixty Years* (Asia Publication House), Bombay, 1965.

101. Nehru Jawaharlal (1943): *India Can Learn from China* (Asia Pub.), America, January, 1993.

102. Nehru Jawaharlal (1943): *The Architect of Modern India*, Anande Goplal Mukherjee & Tangra Vinod Reliance Pub.

103. Nayar, Deepak (1995): *Globalisation: The Past in Our Present*, I.E.A. Presidential Address.

104. Nagraj, R. (1990): "Growth Rate of India's G.D.P. 1950-51 to 1987-88. Examination of Alternation of Alternative Hypothesis," *Economic and Political Weekly*, June.

105. Nehru, Jawaharlal (1956): *The Discovery of India*, Meridian Books, London, 1956, 4th Edition.

106. Nandi, B.R. (1961): *The Nehrus: Motilal and Jawaharlal* (Allen & Unwin), London.

107. Narsimbhih, C.D. (1960): *India's Spokesman, Speeches and Addresses of Jawaharlal Nehru* (Mc Millan & Co.), Madras.

108. Rao, V.K.R.V. (1966): *Essays in Economic Development* (Asia Publishing House), Bombay.

109. Rao, V.K.R.V. (1962): *Agricultural Labour in India* (Ed.) (Asia Pub. House), Bombay.

110. Rushbrook, Williams, L.F. (1936): *What About India?*, London.

111. Rao, V.K.R.V. (1985): *New Approach to Indian Planning Some Suggestion* (J. Krishnamachani Memorial Lecture).

112. Rao, V.K.R.V. (1971): *The Nehru Legacy*, Popular Prakashan, Bombay.

113. Rostow, W.W. (1960): *The Stages of Economic Growth* (Cambridge University), London, 1960.

114. *Report to the All India Congress Committee*, 1938, Allahabad.

115. Rohatai, Sushila (1986): *Jawaharlal Nehru as a Parliamentarian* (Lok Sabha Secretariate), New Delhi.

116. Rao, Amity (1974): *Jawaharlal Nehru: Prime Minister* (Sterling Pub.), New Delhi.

117. Jain, S.P. (1959): The Project in a Study of Nehru by Rafique Zakaria (*A Times of India Publication*), 2nd Edn.

118. Prasad, Bimla (1972): *Jawaharlal Nehru's Report on International Congress Against Imperialism* (The Origine of Indian Foreign Policy).

119. Planning Commission, *Human Development Report*, 2002.

120. Planning Commission, *First Five Year Plan to Tenth Five Year Plan.*

121. Planning Commission, *Approach to the Tenth Five Year Plan.*

122. Parikh, Kirti (1997): *Indian Development Report.*

123. Prakash, Shri (1994): Liberalisation of Indian Economy and Relevance of Nehru Mahalanobis strategy of Development A.K. Sinha (Ed.) *New Economic Policy of India,* New Delhi.

124. Parliamentary Library (Lok Sabha Secretariate): *Parliament of India,* 9th, 10th, 11th and 12th Lok Sabha.

125. Kashyap S.C. (1989): *Jawaharlal Nehru and Planning in India* (Lok Sabha Secretariate), New Delhi.

126. Kashyap, S.C. (1989): *Parliament and Humar* (*Ibid.*).

127. Kashyap, S.C. (1989): (*Lok Sabha Secretariate*), New Delhi.

128. Kashyap, S.C. (1989): *Socio-economic Background of Lok Sabha Members* - 10th, 11th and 12th Lok Sabha (Lok Sabha Secretariate).

129. Kashyap, S.C. (1989): *Nehru: A True Democrat* (Lok Sabha Secretariate).

130. Kashyap, S.C. (1990): *Jawaharlal Nehru: His Life Work and Legacy* (Lok Sabha Secretariate).

131. Reddy, Venugopal (1992): *Public Enterprises Reforms and Privatisation* (Deep & Deep Publication, New Delhi).

132. Godan, R. (1996): *Economic Reforms in India* (Deep & Deep Publication), New Delhi.

133. Chandra, S & B. (1998): *Privatisation of Public Enterprises: A Constitutional Antomy* (Deep & Deep Publication), New Delhi.

134. Brahmachari, O.P. (1995): *The Public Sector: Today: New Perspecteive in Economic Reforms* (Deep & Deep Pub.), New Delhi.

135. Beting, G.S. (1995): *Globalisation Strategy and Economic Liberalisation,* Anmol Publications Pvt. Ltd., New Delhi.

136. Shrivastava, S.K. (1970): *History of Economic Thought* (S. Chand & Co.), New Delhi.

137. Shrivastava, M.P. (1986): "Public Unertaking: An Important Tool of Socio-Economic Structure" (*Lok Udyog*), May 1985, Govt. of India, Ministry of Finance, New Delhi.

138. Srivastava, M.P. (1987): *Problem of Accountability of Public Enterprises* (Uppal Publ. House), New Delhi.

139. Srivastava, M.P. (1992): *Capacity Utilisation and Cost of Production* (Deep & Deep Pub.), New Delhi.

140. Srivastava M.P. (1992): *Parliamentary Accountability and Supervision over Public Enterprises* (Deep & Deep Publication), New Delhi.

141. Srivastava, M.P. & Prasad Virendra (1992): *Public Enterprises in India Government Supervision,* Chugh Publication, Allahabad.

142. Srivastava, M.P. & Prasad Virendra (1994): "From GATT to WTO & India" Ed. K.R. Gupta, *World Trade,* Atlantic Publication, New Delhi.

143. Shrivastava, M.P. (2000): *Parliament and Financial Committees,* Anmol Publications Pvt. Ltd., New Delhi.

144. Srivastava, M.P. & Prasad, Virendra (1996): "Socio-Economic Contributions of Jawaharlal Nehru in Present Day Context", *Bhoo-Chintan,* Economic Development Research Institute, Gaya.

145. Srivastava, M.P. & Sahay B.R. (2001): *National Agriculture Policy in the New Millenium* (Anmol Publications Pvt. Ltd., New Delhi).

146. Singer, H. (1997): *Rich and Poor Countries*, George Allen & Unwen, London.

147. Shakdhar, S.L. (1986): Nehru & Presiding Officer, *Nehru and Parliament* (Ed.) S.C. Kashyap (Lok Sabha Secretariate), New Delhi.

148. Shah, K.K. (1986): *Parliamentary Democracy*, Right Means to Achieve Ends. *op. cit.*

149. Singh, V.B. (1977): *Nehru on Socialism*, Govt. of India, (Publication Division), New Delhi.

150. Sarvapalli, Gopal (1976): *Jawaharlal Nehru*, Oxford University Press, Bombay.

151. Sah, A.B. (1965): *Jawaharlal Nehru: A Critical Tributes* (Manaktalas), Bombay.

152. Shenoy, B.R. (1963): *Indian Planning and Economic Development*, Asia Publication, New Delhi.

153. Spencer, Conalia (1951): *Nehru of India*, Phoemix Press, Bangalore.

154. Singh, Baljit (1966): *Economic of Development*, Asia Publication, New Delhi.

155. Singh, Umrao (1962): Community Development in India (Kitab Ghar), Kanpur.

156. Singh, B.N., Shrivastava, Mohan Prasad, Prasad Narendra (2000): *Indian Economic in the Twenty First Century*, Anmol Publications Pvt. Ltd., New Delhi.

157. Singh, B.N., Shrivastava, Mohan Prasad, Prasad Narendra (2003), *Economic Reforms in India*, Anmol Publications Pvt. Ltd., New Dehli

158. Tyson (1966): *Nehru: The Years of Power*, Pall Mall Press, London.

159. Tendulkar, S. & Jain L.R. (1995): "Economic Reforms and Poverty", *Economic Political Weekly*, June, 1995.

Reports

1. World Bank (1966): *World Development Reports.*
2. I.M.F. (1997): *World Economic Out Look,* Washington D.C., May.
3. Lok Sabha Secretariate: *Indian Journal of Parliamentary Information,* Quarterly Journal.
4. *Economic & Political Weekly*, Shahid Bhagat Singh Road, Mumbai.
5. FICCI: Federation House, New Delhi.
6. *Mainstream,* New Delhi.
7. *Kurukshetra,* Publication Division, New Delhi.
8. *Indian Journal of Public Administration,* I.I.P.A., New Delhi.
9. *Indian of Public Enterprise Journal* (I.P.E.J.), Hyderabad.
10. *Indian Institute of Public Enterprises,* Hyderabad.
11. *Indian Economic Journal,* Mumbai.
12. *The Economic Times,* Bombay, Calcutta.
13. *The Times of India.*
14. *The Statesman.*
15. *The Indian Express.*
16. *The Financial Express.*
17. *The Hindu.*
18. *R.B.I. Bulletin.*
19. *Five Year Plans,* (1st Plan to Xth Plan).
20. *Human Development Report 1991-92 to 2002;* Oxford University Press.

21. *Public Enterprises Survey 1991.*

22. *Economic Survey 2001-2002, 2002-03.*

23. *Union Budget,* Government of India from 1991-92 to 2002-2003.

24. *Human Development Report, 2002,* Planning Commission.

25. *World Development Report,* 2002, Oxford University Press.